EASTERN MONTANA'S MOUNTAIN RANGES

Islands on the Prairie

BY MARK MELOY

NUMBER THIRTEEN

MONTANA GEOGRAPHIC SERIES

Text Copyright ©, 1986 by Mark Meloy

PUBLISHED BY

Montana Magazine, Inc.

HELENA, MONTANA

RICK GRAETZ, PUBLISHER
MARK THOMPSON, DIRECTOR OF PUBLICATIONS
BARBARA FIFER, ASSISTANT BOOK EDITOR
CAROLYN CUNNINGHAM, EDITOR—MONTANA MAGAZINE

This series intends to fill the need for in-depth information about Montana subjects. The geographic concept explores the historical color, the huge landscape and the resilient people of a single Montana subject area. All typesetting, design and layout production completed in Helena, Montana. Printed in Japan by DNP America, San Francisco.

preface

The eastern two-thirds of Montana is a huge curve of land broken by random clusters of mountains and stream terraces; an ancient sea bed gently listing toward the jagged folds of the Continental Divide.

Geologists call it the outlier province of the Northern Great Plains. It is separate and distinct, a topographical twilight zone where two distinct geographic regions— plains and mountains— momentarily share the same vast stretch of continent. Isolated mountains rise from the great arid basins of the Yellowstone and Missouri rivers just as the plains merge with the eastern front of the Rocky Mountains. They break the level horizon like mirages of huge ships or islands in the ocean giving measure to the ephemeral blue of distance.

My personal discovery of this unique geographic province began in the Big Snowy Mountains south of Lewistown. At the dead center of Montana, I was told, the crest of the Snowies held a fabled panorama of a dozen distant mountain ranges, rising from the ocean of prairie.

The trailhead began at Crystal Lake, set in a large forested bowl on the Snowies' north flank. With loaded backpack, I headed for the crest along a steep switchback trail. Darkness was on my heels as I emerged from the timberland slopes to the open meadow on top. I nestled my tent into the thick grasses of alpine prairie.

The next day I ambled up Knife Blade Ridge to the summit of Great

the soft caress of evening light the extraordinary view emerged: far-off islands in the prairie ocean, 300 miles distant of one another, the crags of the Absarokas rose to the south, and the Sweetgrass Hills bordered the north horizon. In between, mountains were scattered across the prairie in all directions: the Bearpaws, Crazies, Moccasins, Judiths, Highwoods, Castles, Bighorns, Pryors, Bulls, Little Rockies and Beartooths.

The prairie sunset deepened the panorama in lavender shadows. Darkness erased the border between earth and sky, and random farm lights mixed with sparkling stars, giving me the sensation of being set adrift with no earthly reference but the patch of ground beneath my feet.

In the morning, the gossamer waves of early light spread across the terraces of the Musselshell River to the south. The hills and gullies of the plain fanned out from the Little Belts to the Bull Mountains, from Judith Gap to Roundup, a landscape etched by occasional roads and thin lines of streambeds marked by shadows. The undulate prairie seemed to lap my exquisite mountain palace like ocean waves against an exotic island.

That was my initial view of the prairie outliers, all together, seen from afar. My work on this book allowed me to fulfill a wish of that summer evening, to view each range more closely— its history, communities and natural attractions.

contents

Montana Magazine, Inc. ▬▬▬▬▬
Box 5630
Helena, Montana 59604   ISBN 0-938314-24-6

ACKNOWLEDGEMENTS: ▬▬▬▬▬
The writing of this book was a family project. Without the editorial
genius of my wife, Ellen, and the research assistance so generously
provided by my mother, Harriett Meloy, former research librarian
at the Montana Historical Society, this book might not have been
accomplished. Heartfelt gratitude goes to the Montana families who
told of their beloved mountains that these pages might fairly
represent and share the romance of that landscape.

ABOUT THE AUTHOR: ▬▬▬▬▬
A third generation Montanan, Mark Meloy is a writer-
photographer from Helena. When not rambling backroads in search
of the perfect sunset, he will be found on a ladder refurbishing
homes in the capital city.

Highwood Mountains at sunset from the Judith Basin near Danvers. TOM DIETRICH

14643

introduction

On a cleary day you can stand almost anywhere in central Montana and imagine the distant mountains to be an archipelago of islands floating in the sea of the Northern Plains. The flat or gently rolling grasslands are broken by abrupt rises of land, some craggy, others gentle, all flanked by forest or shrub vegetation that marks an abrupt edge in height and color between plain and mountain.

Some of the island ranges are mirror images of the mainstem Rockies, ecological microcosms of the Continental Divide. Others are hybrids of alpine and prairie habitat: rolling, dry ranges—more of a low-slung rise than a mountain range in the classic—sense forested by drought-resistant shrubs, grasses and conifers. Some are highland features, a gathering of buttes, broken stream terraces or the high ground between the erosion tables of two rivers, places that harbor unique canyonlands and desert environments.

The drainages of the two great rivers of eastern Montana, the Yellowstone and the Missouri, form the larger boundaries of the outlier province. North of the Missouri are the Hi-Line ranges: the Sweetgrass Hills, Bearpaws and Little Rocky Mountains. The southern half of the Missouri Basin contains the mountains of central Montana: the Little Belt, Castle, Highwood, Moccasin, Judith and Snowy mountains. In the third area are the Yellowstone Basin ranges: the Crazy, Bull, Pryor, Bighorn, Sheep and Wolf mountains and the highland features of the Tongue River Breaks, the Long Pines and Chalk Buttes.

Though some of the outliers are simply high terraces of erosion, most of them were created by enormous mountain-building convolutions below the earth's surface 50 million years ago. In an event that puzzles geologists, molten rock intruded from the fiery mantle of the earth and hardened in the bulging sedimentary rock near the surface. Subsequent erosion carved the igneous blisters into mountains bordering the larger plains of the great rivers. These laccoliths—literally "lakes of rock"—are the underground plumbing of volcanoes. To geologists, this profusion of laccoliths clustered around a relatively small area of the earth's surface is remarkable.

The island ranges harbor diverse communities of mountain-loving plants and animals seeking sanctuary from the arid, largely treeless prairie. Since most of the mountain islands capture more rainfall than the surrounding prairies, they maintain an environment similar to the Rockies. A few of the ranges support nearly the entire spectrum of Western flora and fauna in habitats that range from moist alpine meadow to desert soils nearly devoid of vegetation—all in an area of fewer than 20 miles. The isolated ranges have been studied as "habitat islands" in much the same way as Charles Darwin first looked at the Galapagos Islands of the Pacific Ocean.

Water is the common denominator for all forms of life on the arid prairie. Central and eastern Mon-

tana are largely dependent on agriculture which, in turn, derives its life-giving force from the water captured by and shed from these mountains.

The region's white pioneer societies evolved from trading posts and mining camps established in or near the mountains, close to the resources people so eagerly sought. Such settlements were among the earliest located away from the frontier river ports on the Yellowstone and Missouri. Eventually those settlers fanned out from the mountains to pursue more stable occupations in farming and ranching. The exploitation of mountain resources —timber, minerals, water, wildlife and recreation—then continued generally on a seasonal basis. As transportation improved, it was reasonable to go to the mountains in the summer, but live in the relatively benign winter environments of the prairie river valleys.

Despite the scars of historic and recent mining and 20th-century timber harvests, the prairie ranges remain relatively free of development. Used primarily as summer pastures for livestock from the valleys, they have retained much of the wilderness flavor experienced by those who first explored them.

Today hordes of people from Montana's growing urban centers flock to the mountains for recreation. In many respects that recreation is an attempt to relive the frontier adventure of those who established new lives in the pristine wilderness. People look to the mountains for simple relief from the dry, even prairies—a picnic, a hike or a chance to fill the freezer with elk and venison.

Russell Point in the Little Belt Mountains
BILL KOENIG

Perhaps most important, the mountains are geographic landmarks, symbols of home to those who live around them. The sight of the mountain landscape, the measured blue distance beyond one's fences, is one of the intangibles that makes life in Montana unique and enriching.

Ask a Montanan for directions. More often than not, you'll get an answer with the name of a mountain range in it: "Over the backside of the Bearpaws" or "in the Judith Gap between the Little Belts and Snowies" or "out on the desert below the Pryors." The outliers anchor peoples' lives to the open prairie.

Above: Sweetgrass Creek in the Crazy Mountains. MARK MELOY
Left: Rainshower over the Big Snowy Mountains near Glengarry. TOM DIETRICH
Below: The abandoned smelter at Zortman in the Little Rocky Mountains. ROBERT BREWER

geology: Mountains

by Dave Alt

Don't confuse them with the Rocky Mountains. The scattered mountains east of the Rocky Mountain front in central and eastern Montana are completely different. Some, such as the Bull Mountains, are simply patches of rugged hills eroded into resistant bedrock, not really mountains in the geologic sense of the word. Others are the genuine article, big folds in the earth's crust, old volcanoes, massive igneous intrusions. The crustal movements happened and the magmas melted for unknown reasons that probably had nothing to do with the Rocky Mountains.

Dave Alt is a professor of geology at the University of Montana, a columnist in Montana Magazine *and a contributor to several books in the Montana Geographic Series.*

Sedimentary formations in the Little Belts are riddled with caves such as this one called Window Rock . BILL KOENIG

COAL HILLS

Let's start with those scattered patches of hills eroded into hard bedrock. They seem always to coincide with coal country, so I will call them coal hills. They are a major and altogether lovely part of the landscape of Montana east of the Rocky Mountains.

In addition to the Bull Mountains between Roundup and Billings, the coal hills include the big tracts of rugged country near Lame Deer, Colstrip and Broadus, and many lesser patches of steep and colorful hills here and through much of eastern Montana. They are eroded into massive beds of resistant sandstone in the upper part of the Fort Union formation, the part that contains most of the coal. Thick beds of sandstone tend to erode into rugged hills and the coal helps make those hills colorful as well as rugged.

A seam of coal under a layer of sandstone near Fattig Creek in the Bull Mountains.
MARK MELOY

Top: The Snowy Mountains south of Lewistown are literally a blister or a bubble of rock injected between rock strata, the top layers of which have since disappeared. JIM ROMO
Bottom: The Pryor Mountains east of Billings are a fold in the earth's crust. This is from Dry Head Vista. CHARLES KAY

As soon as streams erode their beds deeply enough to drain the ground water out of a coal seam, it dries out. Then, eventually, lightning or range fire ignites the coal. Once lit, the fire smolders for centuries, if the coal seam lasts that long, until it finally runs out of fuel. Many coal seams burn right through the hill to the next stream valley. It is no accident that the mines tend to be in low areas where the coal is still too full of water to burn.

Coal burns hot, thoroughly baking the sandstone and mudstone above it to the color, hardness and erosion-resistance of kiln-fired brick. Many people call that coal-fired rock *scoria*, but clinker is probably a better word. It is an important resource in eastern Montana, where rocks hard enough to make good road material are rare. Watch for the red roads. And those coal-baked rocks help make the coal hills rugged, give the ridge crests their colorful caps and paint red and orange bands along the sides of the ridges. Each band of bright color in this landscape records a burned coal seam.

ARCHES IN THE PLAINS

Many of the ranges east of the Rocky Mountains consist basically of big folds arched in the high plains. Quite a few of those folds tilt the Fort Union formation, the big accumulation of sediments that contains most of the coal in central and eastern Montana. Some of the layers of sand and mud in the Fort Union formation were still accumulating as recently as 55 million years ago, so we can be sure that the crustal movements that tilted them happened sometime since then. Other sedimentary rocks laid down as much as 35 million years ago are much less tilted, so the folds must have formed sometime between 55 and 35 million years ago. Fifty million years ago is a reasonably good number.

Little Belt Mountains

The Little Belt Mountains southeast of Great Falls are another steep arch in the plains, complicated by a number of faults that shoved the rocks generally eastward. Those structures bring ancient basement rocks of the continental crust to the surface in the area near Neihart. Other rocks exposed in the center of the Little Belt Mountains are the older sedimentary formations that cover the basement and lie deeply buried in most of the region.

The northern part of the Little Belt Mountains contains a beautiful set of igneous intrusions, mostly varieties of syenite, neatly arranged around a common center almost as though they were on the rim of a wheel. Each large intrusion is approximately circular. Each lies at the end of a dike, a fracture filled with igneous rock, that appears to have been the conduit that fed magma into the intrusion.

Snowy Mountains

The Big Snowy Mountains and their eastward extension in the Little Snowy Mountains are directly south of Lewistown. They look from a distance like what they are: a broad dome with very gently sloping flanks, a blister in the plains. The geologic map shows that the dome is slightly elliptical, with its long axis pointing east. Erosion has stripped the younger formations from the top of the arch, exposing older rocks that we could otherwise see only in cores taken from deep wells. Another few million years of erosion will expose basement rocks in the southern part of the Big Snowy mountains. Some of the sedimentary formations we see there now produce oil and gas from the crests of other folds that are still deeply buried.

Pryor Mountains

The Pryor Mountains are another broad arch in the high plains, the low northern end of the high Bighorn Range of Wyoming. The most conspicuous rock exposed in the Pryor Mountains is the Madison limestone, a section of massive limestone between 1,000 and 200 feet thick in most areas and so pale gray that it is almost white. Most people get their closest view of the Pryor Mountains in the Bighorn Canyon recreation area. The towering cliffs that rise above the river there are pale gray Madison limestone. As everywhere, the Madison limestone here is full of fossils, including large coral heads, the remains of tropical animals that must have lived in shallow sea water.

Cedar Creek Anticline

The Cedar Creek anticline is a very steep folded arch that trends from just west of Glendive slightly south of east through Baker, and into South Dakota. It is probably no accident that the trend is parallel to the folds that form the Bridger Range, the Bighorn Mountains of Wyoming and the Black Hills of South Dakota. The Cedar Creek anticline almost certainly formed as a fault broke the continental crust on which the sedimentary rocks beneath the plains were draped like a blanket.

In geologic principle, the Cedar Creek anticline should rank among the mountains of eastern Montana. As it happens, the older rocks that surface in the crest of the fold are hardly more resistant to erosion than the younger formations nearby. So they don't stand up in erosional relief to form a line of hills. But the Cedar Creek anticline is important to the economy of Montana, even if not to the landscape, because it trapped large amounts of petroleum to form an almost continuous line of oil and gas fields along its crest.

IGNEOUS CENTERS

Most of the mountains in central Montana involve igneous rocks that crystallized from molten magma. In three big ranges, the Adel, Highwood and Bearpaw mountains, the magmas erupted to form volcanoes, probably clusters of volcanoes. In the others, the magma crystallized before it reached the surface to form igneous intrusions.

It is possible to measure the ages of igneous rocks by analyzing their contents of parent radioactive elements, and comparing those to the amounts of the daughter elements formed through radioactive decay. In essence, that is the same as determining how long an hourglass has been running by comparing the amount of sand on the bottom with that still on top. Such age dates show that most of the igneous rocks east of the Rocky Mountain front

The Cedar Creek Anticline, which accounts for much of the badland topography around Baker, is simply a fault or break in the surface rock that allowed differential erosion of the exposed strata.

The Highwood Mountains were active volcanoes 50 million years ago. MARK THOMPSON

formed about 50 million years ago, give or take 5 million years. That is about the same answer we get by looking at the ages of the folded sedimentary formations.

THREE VOLCANIC CENTERS

The old volcanic piles of the Adel, Highwood and Bearpaw mountains, from southwest to northeast, line up along a nearly straight trend. All three centers were active sometime around 50 million years ago, perhaps a little earlier in the Adel Mountains. All three began their careers by erupting fairly normal lava, then finished by producing large volumes of an extremely unusual rock, a central Montana specialty called shonkinite, after Shonkin Creek in the Highwood Mountains.

Shonkinite consists essentially of two basic rock-forming minerals: white potassium feldspar and augite, which is black. The color of the augite dominates to make a very dark rock. The potassium content of shonkinite is typically several times that of ordinary dark igneous rocks. Laboratory experiments show that shonkinite magma must melt somewhere deep within the earth, probably at least 200 miles below the surface, but no one knows exactly how, why or where it forms.

Although most of the shonkinite magma erupted to form volcanic rocks, some crystallized below the surface to form igneous intrusions. Many of the shonkinite intrusions are laccoliths that formed as blisters of magma injected between sedimentary layers to make an intrusion shaped about like a Vanilla Wafer.

In some laccoliths, the original shonkinite magma separated after it was intruded to form a thin cap of white syenite composed almost entirely of potassium feldspar that rests on a much thicker layer of dark shonkinite. For many years, most geologists thought that the cap of white syenite formed as growing crystals of potassium feldspar floated upward through the shonkinite magma. Recent research makes it seem more likely that molten syenite separated from the original shonkinite magma and floated to the top of the laccolith about the way cream separates from milk.

Adel Mountains

Although they huddle so close to the Rocky Mountain front that they seem like part of the Rockies, the Adel Mountains really belong to central Montana. Interstate 15 passes through them southwest of Great Falls, between Cascade and Wolf Creek. Watch for dark shonkinite exposed in roadcuts and in the Missouri River canyon. Three Sisters Mountain, in the hills south of the river about 12 miles south of Cascade, is the deeply eroded ruin of the volcano that erupted most of the original pile of volcanic rocks.

People who travel Highway 200 west of Great Falls pass three large northern outposts of the Adel Mountains: Square, Shaw and Crown buttes, a parade of flat-topped sentinels south of the road between Sun River and Simms. All are laccoliths, blisters of shonkinite injected as molten magma between layers of sedimentary rock. Cascade Butte is another. Now, 50 million or more years of erosion later, the resistant shonkinite stands in high relief after the much softer sedimentary rocks that once enclosed it have eroded away.

Each of those buttes is at the north end of a big dike, a fracture filled with igneous rock. Those were the fractures that fed molten magma into the laccoliths. Side roads between Fort Shaw and Cascade pass those dikes. They look like the ruins of great walls laid out across the prairie in almost perfectly straight lines radiating from Three Sisters Mountain at the geologic center of the Adel Mountains about 15 miles to the north.

The steep cliffs that surround Crown Butte effectively protect its flat top from all but the most determined visitors. The plant species there are remnants of the original prairie that covered all the region when Lewis and Clark came through. This country never was grazed and is preserved almost perfectly. Atop Square Butte is another island of almost undisturbed prairie.

Highwood Mountains

The rugged Highwood Mountains that punctuate the skyline east of Great Falls are a big volcanic pile that probably erupted from several centers, including Highwood Peak. Fifty million or so years of erosion have dissected the original volcanic landscape almost beyond recognition. But the rocks, mostly shonkinite, leave no doubt that these mountains were indeed a cluster of volcanoes.

The Shonkin Sag, an abandoned valley broad enough to hold a river bigger than the modern Missouri, cuts right through the northern part of the Highwood Mountains. During at least one of the great ice ages, it was the spillway that carried overflow from Glacial Lake Great Falls, a vast inland sea that backed up behind the ice in the general area between Great Falls and Shelby. A row of shallow lakes in the valley floor is all that remains to tell us of the muddy torrents that roared through this valley during warm ice-age summers.

Square Butte and Round Butte, a pair of extremely large laccoliths, are the easternmost outposts of the Highwood Mountains. They rise like a gigantic pair of gnarled stumps west of Highway 80 between Geraldine and Square Butte, the caps of syenite gleaming white above the dark shonkinite below.

Bearpaw Mountains

The scattered clumps of rugged hills that together make the Bearpaw Mountains sprawl across a vast region south of Havre, east of Highway 87. A body of rock called the Rocky Boy stock, near Rocky Boy, is certainly the deeply eroded core of one of the original volcanoes. Surely there were others; a single volcano seems unable to have spread lava over such a large area. Here, too, 50 million years of erosion have so deeply carved the original volcanoes that it is impossible to recognize them in the landscape.

In addition to volcanic rocks, the Bearpaw Mountains include quite a number of intrusions, most of them laccoliths. Box Elder Butte, directly east of Box Elder, is one of the largest and most conspicuous. It wears a cap of gleaming white syenite that is visible from Highway 87. Snake Butte, an isolated outpost northeast of the main mass of the Bearpaws, is another laccolith, also with a cap of white syenite. A quarry in the side of Snake Butte provided the big blocks of black shonkinite that were used for riprap on the Fort Peck Dam.

The Bearpaw Mountains stand on the crest of a broad arch gently warped in the rocks of the High Plains, the Bearpaw uplift. Wells in the big Tiger Ridge gas field south of Havre draw from enormous quantities of natural gas trapped in the crest of that arch.

Top: Square Butte near Box Elder is blister of rock called a laccolith. JIM ROMO
Bottom: The town of Stockett is on the bed of an ancient channel that contained what is now the Missouri River. JOHN REDDY

Crazy Mountains

People who travel Interstate 90 between Livingston and Billings see the glaciated peaks, snowcapped most of the year, of the southern Crazy Mountains looming in the north. Those same peaks make a splendid backdrop east of Highway 89 to the north of Livingston, west of Highway 191 to the north of Big Timber. It is a spectacular range. Farther north, the Crazy Mountains become much lower and break into groups of forested hills.

The core of the southern Crazy Mountains is a large igneous intrusion called the Big Timber stock, which invaded the Fort Union formation sometime around 50 million years ago. The Fort Union formation was only a few million years old then and it was still soft, a thick pile of watery sands and muds. The magma must have risen very close to the surface and may have erupted. But no volcanic rocks survive.

The Fort Union formation buckled into a broad arch as the magma rose. Cracks opened along the length of the fold, then filled with molten magma to form spectacular swarms of dikes, many of them 50 or more feet thick, that extend north and south of the main intrusion. Like so many large dikes, these look like old walls running straight across the hills and valleys. They reach several miles north and south of the intrusion in the core of the range.

It must have been a steamy time when that red-hot magma rose into the watery sediments of the Fort Union formation. Heat escaping from the magma drove the water from the soft sediments and baked them into hard rock. During the last 50 million years, the soft sandstones and mudstones of the un-altered Fort Union formation have eroded away, leaving the more resistant igneous intrusion with its surroundings of baked and altered sedimentary rocks standing up in relief. That is why the southern Crazy Mountains are so high.

The southern Crazy Mountains are among the few ranges in central Montana that caught enough snow to support large glaciers during the ice ages. Even now, those high peaks clothe themselves in snow most of the year. The gnarled peaks that rise steeply from deeply-gouged valleys make one of the most spectacular alpine landscapes in Montana.

The low hills of the northern Crazy Mountains are a swarm of small igneous intrusions into the Fort Union formation. Like the much larger intrusion in the southern Crazy Mountains, most of those in the northern part of the range also baked and altered the Fort Union formation near their contacts. The largest and northernmost intrusion in the Crazy Mountains is Gordon Butte, just south of Martinsdale on Highway 12. It is an almost perfectly circular laccolith more than 500 feet thick. The intrusion sagged into a saucer shape as the weight of the magma compressed the soft Fort Union formation beneath it.

Rough country of Square Butte. The dark pinnacles in the foreground are a rock called Shonkinite, an eastern Montana specialty named for Shonkin Creek in the Highwood Mountains. The white cliffs are syenite. The way in which the two occur is of great interest to geologists.
DON HYNDMAN

THE INTRUSIVE CENTERS

The Judith and Moccasin mountains, the Sweetgrass Hills, the Little Rocky Mountains, the Little Belt Mountains, Castle Mountain and scattered isolated buttes all consist of large and complex masses of light-colored igneous rocks that crystallized below the surface to form intrusions. All of those centers contain little or no volcanic rock, so it seems that the igneous rocks crystallized almost entirely at depth.

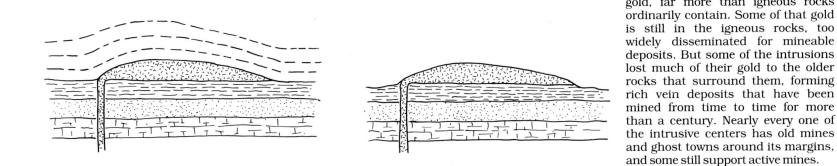

Diagram: Magma rises along a vertical fracture, then spreads horizontally between sedimentary layers to form what is called a laccolith, attached to a dike. Later erosion strips off the soft sedimentary rock to expose the igneous rock of the laccolith.

Photo: Black Butte on the north end of the Judith Mountains is a good example of a laccolith. MARK MELOY

The typical rock of those intrusions consists of large and blocky crystals of feldspar scattered through a matrix of microscopic crystals of feldspar, quartz and a variety of black minerals. Technically, the rocks go under several names: granite, syenite, monzonite, and so forth. Syenite, a pale rock composed almost entirely of feldspar and lacking quartz, is the most common. Despite the confusing terminology, most of the different rocks closely resemble each other. They are slight variations on a common theme.

Most of those magmas, by whatever name, contained quite a lot of gold, far more than igneous rocks ordinarily contain. Some of that gold is still in the igneous rocks, too widely disseminated for mineable deposits. But some of the intrusions lost much of their gold to the older rocks that surround them, forming rich vein deposits that have been mined from time to time for more than a century. Nearly every one of the intrusive centers has old mines and ghost towns around its margins, and some still support active mines.

Judith and Moccasin Mountains

The Judith Mountains are a tight cluster of igneous intrusions. Each formed when a big glob of molten magma rose to within a couple of thousand feet of the earth's surface, then crystallized. If any of those intrusions erupted, there is no evidence of it in the form of volcanic rocks. If you had been living in the area of the Judith Mountains 50 million years ago, you probably would have seen the ground surface swell into a large bulge during a period of several months as each intrusion rose into position. Erosion has since stripped off most of the cover of sedimentary formations to expose the hard igneous rocks and create the rugged landscape that we see today.

The geologic maps of the Judith Mountains show some fascinating structures. Several of the masses of molten magma popped their covers of older sedimentary rocks like big trapdoors, then squeezed out of the crack. Now we see the igneous intrusions in all stages of erosional exposure. Some have completely lost their original sedimentary cover, others peep out from under their lids of sedimentary rocks. Still other igneous intrusions remain unexposed and appear as broad bulges

Middle Butte in the Sweetgrass Hills.
MARK MELOY

in the landscape. Watch for those along Highway 87 east of Lewistown.

The Moccasin Mountains are a matched pair of two large buttes that stand distinctly west of the main mass of the Judith Mountains, but not far enough apart to seem really separate. Black Butte is another such outpost northeast of the main cluster of the Judith Mountains. Each contains in its core large intrusions composed of varieties of syenite and granite.

The molten magmas that made the Judith and Moccasin Mountains brought large quantities of gold with them to form ore bodies in and near the igneous intrusions. Mining began more than a century ago and has continued off and on ever since, whenever the price of gold was high. The old towns of Maiden and Gilt Edge in the Judiths and Kendall in North Moccasin Butte were once thriving little cities. Old mine dumps are about all that survive.

Sweetgrass Hills

The Sweetgrass Hills north of Shelby consist mainly of East, Middle and West buttes, each a self-contained miniature mountain range. The three big buttes of the Sweetgrass Hills are almost identical in every geologic respect to the two Moccasin buttes west of the Judith Mountains. Each big butte has its core of igneous intrusions, mostly varieties of syenite. Sedimentary rocks dragged up by the rising magma wrap around the igneous cores. As in so many of the mountains of central Montana, the Madison limestone is the most conspicuous sedimentary formation. It forms high ridges and cliffs of gleaming white rock that surround the much younger igneous intrusions.

Middle Butte rightly also is called Gold Butte, and East Butte has its share of old mines, too. For some unexplained reason, West Butte is one of the few large syenite intrusions in central Montana that contains no gold.

The Sweetgrass Hills also include two smaller hills, Grassy and Haystack buttes. They are examples of the smaller and extremely peculiar igneous intrusions called diatremes that abound in central Montana. Diatremes consist of various kinds of dark and heavy igneous rocks that could have come only from deep beneath the earth's crust, perhaps hundreds of miles down. They come in various shapes, but most are like cylinders a few hundred feet in diameter, stabbed vertically through the earth's crust. The rocks in most diatremes tend to weather easily, so it is rare to find them resisting erosion well enough to stand up as prominent buttes. A few Montana diatremes contain sapphires. Quite a few in other parts of the world contain diamonds, but none have been found so far in Montana.

Little Rocky Mountains

The Little Rocky Mountains, south of the High Line near Harlem, are a circular uplift so sharply punched into the high plains that it looks as though a giant piston might have driven it up from below. In fact, something like that may actually have happened. A large group of syenite intrusions in the center of the range suggests that a much larger body of igneous rock may exist at depth, and may have driven the rocks up as it intruded the basement rocks below.

Twin Lakes at the head of Big Timber Canyon in the Crazy Mountains.
MARK MELOY

Steeply tilted beds of Madison limestone, a formation more than 1,000 feet thick, encircle the Little Rocky Mountains. Limestone resists erosion in the dry climate of central Montana, so the Madison formation stands up in bold relief as though it were an enormous wall. From a distance, and in the dim light of early morning or late evening, it is easy to imagine the Little Rocky Mountains as the rubble of an ancient city of giants, standing within the ruins of its great wall.

The center of the Little Rocky Mountains consists mostly of 50-million-year-old igneous rock, syen-

Left: The layer-cake nature of much of eastern Montana's sedimentary rock can be seen in this feature near Conrad called "The Knees." JOHN REDDY
Below: Driven up from deep in the earth, the Little Rockies contain valuable minerals. CHARLES KAY

ite, along with some basement rock. At least some of the basement rock appears to be large blocks that were dragged up with the rising magma. Like most of the syenite intrusions in central Montana, this one brought large quantities of gold with it. Mines near Zortman and Landusky in the southern part of the Little Rocky Mountains have produced gold for more than a century, when the price was right.

Castle Mountain

Castle Mountain, southeast of White Sulphur Springs and just north of the Crazy Mountains, is a large intrusion composed mostly of granite and similar rocks. And there are small masses of dark rocks, too. The granite is so deeply weathered and covered with soil that good exposures are few. But the widely scattered outcrops are easy to find because they form spires that look in the dim light of dusk like ruined medieval embattlements rising above the trees. That is how the mountain got its name.

The geologic map of Castle Mountain looks like a target with the granite bullseye surrounded by rings of steeply tilted sedimentary formations. The rising mass of magma dragged them up as it punched through the earth's crust like a blunt stake driven through a stack of paper. Those sedimentary formations include the Madison limestone, which makes big white outcrops.

Volcanic rocks on the north side of Castle Mountain have the same composition as the granite. They leave no doubt that the main mass of molten granitic magma erupted, that a volcano developed on the broad bulge that formed as the big mass of granitic magma approached the surface. Erosion has since stripped off most of the volcano, as well as the roof of sedimentary rocks that once covered the granite, and is now biting deeply into the granite itself.

Instead of gold, the magma that became the Castle Mountain granite imported large amounts of lead and silver, and some copper, into the upper part of the earth's crust. Mines near the old towns of Lennep and Castle worked vein deposits in the sedimentary rocks around the intrusion. According to some accounts, the prospector who discovered those deposits found pebbles of ore in the gravel along the Musselshell River, then traced them some 40 miles upstream to their source in Castle Mountain.

Diagram: Cross-section of Castle Mountain. Granite magma probably penetrated along fault (arrow).

Left: Castle Mountains. JIM ROMO

ecology:

by Larry S. Thompson

One afternoon many years ago, I was loaded into the station wagon with an entourage of neighborhood kids and taken to the matinee— a science fiction thriller based on a story by Sir Arthur Conan Doyle. In the movie, a team of zoologists stumble into a lost world deep in the unknown reaches of the upper Amazon. Their discovery is a towering, isolated butte which, they said, had been "cut off from the march of time by its unscalable cliffs." Because of its isolation, it still supports a community of dinosaurs, ptero-dactyls, giant spiders and other Mesozoic horrors. It is an evolutionary air pocket where relics of the distant past had

Life on an island can be studied in the isolated ranges of eastern Montana just as on an ocean isle. Shown here is an unnamed foothill in the Bearpaw Mountains. ROBERT BREWER

Larry Thompson is a biologist living in Helena. He has written numerous technical and popular articles, and is the author of Montana's Explorers: The Pioneer Naturalists 1805 - 1864, *No. Nine in the Montana Geographic Series,*

the Web of Life in the Islands on the Plain

maintained a toehold by virtue of their complete isolation. The notion of such a lost world seemed plausible at the time, and it became firmly embedded in my young imagination.

A decade later I was driving eastward through the monotonous wheat desert of the Hi-Line. It had been an hour since the highway had left the verdure of Glacier National Park, and my gaze followed the rolling patchwork of dryland strip farms to the murky horizon.

Suddenly an image leapt straight out of my subconscious: a towering, isolated butte in the distance, cloaked in green. A forested island in a sea of rippling grass and grain, its massive shoulders shaggy with firs, its head shrouded in mystery. This was my first view of West Butte, one of the Sweetgrass Hills.

Flashing back as it did to a powerful childhood impression, the image was a strong one. As soon as I could, I began studying a set of contour maps. I discovered that central Montana was virtually an archipelago of forested mountain "islands"—isolated not by sheer cliffs and tropical jungles as in Doyle's story, but by hundreds of miles of uninterrupted strip farms, rangeland and dry, wind-swept prairie.

I vowed to spend time in the islands of the plains and to try my best to unravel their story. Not that I really expected to encounter lumbering Cretaceous relics trapped in an evolutionary backwater—but I was certain that this "lost world" had some surprises in store.

I was not to be disappointed.

These island mountain ranges, it turned out, yielded abundant relics of the distant past—a bit more subtle than battling dinosaurs, but genuine nonetheless.

Birds of prey such as this merlin are particularly important in balancing populations of small rodents in island environments. LARRY THOMPSON

Above: The Crazy Mountains — exotic alpine conditions in an isolated range on the prairie. This is Grasshopper Glacier.
Left: Patches of Mountain Avens on the crest of the Big Snowy Mountains hug the ground to limit exposure to the elements.
LARRY THOMPSON PHOTOS

Inland Islands

The isolated peaks of central Montana are, in fact, an inland archipelago, islands in a sea of grassland. The basin and range country in Nevada and adjacent states is the only other example of such an island system on the continent.

Biologically, an island is anything that is surrounded by a barrier. Despite our usual image, water is not the only possible barrier to the dispersal of plant and animal species. Like the ocean surrounding a Pacific island, the grasslands of the northern Great Plains also act as a barrier to species that are not adapted to grassland habitats, particularly to montane species— that is, those species adapted to life in moist, forested mountains. Ecologists call the island ranges of the Plains habitat islands— isolated patches of montane habitat (that is, relatively moist, steep, forested habitat similar to that of the main Rocky Mountain ranges) surrounded by a very dissimilar habitat: in this case, semi-arid grassland.

Biologically, an island is anything that is surrounded by a barrier. Despite our usual image, water is not the only possible barrier to the dispersal of plant and animal species. Like the ocean surrounding a Pacific island, the grasslands of the northern Great Plains also act as a barrier to species that are not adapted to grassland habitats, particularly to montane species— that is, those species adapted to life in moist, forested mountains. Ecologists call the island ranges of the Plains habitat islands— isolated patches of montane habitat (that is, relatively moist, steep, forested habitat similar to that of the main Rocky Mountain ranges) surrounded by a very dissimilar habitat: in this case, semi-arid grassland.

Since islands are isolated, they tend to harbor fewer species and lower densities of plants and animals than areas of comparable size and habitat on the mainland. Relatively few species can survive a trip across a wide water barrier. A water barrier is of course most effective for species that cannot fly, do not swim or cannot be carried across the water by winds. Even some of these species, however, can make it across the barrier by "rafting." They hitch a ride on logs or other buoyant vegetation and are carried to a distant island. In some respects, grassland is an even more effective barrier to some species since, unlike water, it allows no possibility for rafting.

Ecologists have studied oceanic islands for many decades. Besides the unique forms that frequently occur on long-isolated oceanic islands, ecologists are also interested in the number and variety of species that occur on islands. The relatively few species found on islands often make up odd communities, far different from anything on the nearest mainland. For example, New Zealand and the Galapagos and Hawaiian islands support no species of native ground-dwelling mammals. In their absence, birds have taken over many of the jobs (niches) that normally would be filled by mammal species. Ecologists are very much interested in explaining why some islands have more species than others, and why the communities of plants and animals on islands— so strikingly different from those on the mainland— are the way they are.

One of the breakthroughs in understanding the patterns of life on islands was the equilibrium theory of island biogeography, first formulated in 1963 by Robert MacArthur of Princeton University and E.O. Wilson of Harvard University. Stated simply, this theory explains that the number of species on a particular island is an equilibrium, or balance, between repeated colonizations and extinctions. Anything that changes the rate at which new species arrive on the island (the colonization rate) or the rate at which they die off from the island (the extinction rate) will affect the number of species found on the island.

The primary influences on the colonization rate are obvious. Clearly, distance from the mainland is important. A potential colonist would have a much better chance of reaching an island fairly close to shore than one miles out to sea. The size of the island also is important. A larger island offers a larger "target area" that increases the chances

that a colonist will reach it. Also, the presence of other islands providing stepping stones from the mainland can increase the colonization rate.

The primary influence on extinction rate is simply the size of the island. A very small island can support only a small population. Environmental change, such as a spell of bad weather, food crop failure or an outbreak of disease, can wipe out the entire population. On a large island, the overall population size is greater, and there is a greater chance that some individuals will be resistant to the change and that at least part of the population will be spared disaster.

How do the islands of the Plains compare to oceanic islands in terms of the numbers of species inhabiting ranges of different sizes and degrees of isolation? Does the logic of the equilibrium theory hold true for these montane islands? Do they harbor any unique forms of plant or animal life as a result of their isolation? The answers to these questions are quite unexpected.

Beginning in 1972, I spent two summers in the islands of the Plains, trapping mammals, counting birds, collecting plants and land snails. Most of my time during those unforgettable months was spent in the Sweetgrass Hills, but I spent many days hiking and exploring the other montane outliers, attempting to unravel part of the mystery of island biogeography. Since then I have returned to these lonely outposts as often as I could, partly to continue studying the flora and fauna, in part just to re-experience the magical sensation of being on a lonely Pacific isle.

Topographic maps show the islands of the plains as a "fringing archipelago"— that is, a group of

Top: The Pryor Mountains offer a nearly desert environment to tough plants such as black sage (foreground) and mountain mahogany.
Bottom: A long-tailed weasel in winter coat.
LARRY THOMPSON PHOTOS

Clark's Nutcracker

Above: Clark's Nutcracker.
Above right: Its favorite food, nuts of the whitebark pine.
LARRY THOMPSON PHOTOS

A hiker in any of the larger ranges of the outlier province is likely to be followed through the woods by a small flock of raucous, fearless birds: the Clark's nutcrackers. Restricted to high, forested mountainous habitats where their preferred food—the nuts of conifers—can be found in abundance, they are only weakly migratory, moving from the high peaks to adjacent valleys in the fall and back to the high country in late winter when breeding occurs. Nevertheless, they have managed to colonize all of the larger montane islands of the plains and are one of the most conspicuous and charac-

teristic birds of these isolated montane habitats.

The Clark's nutcracker's favorite food is the nuts of the whitebark pine, a high-mountain species remarkable in that it occurs in many of the island mountains. The nutcrackers have made a good choice, as anyone who has tasted these mountain morsels can attest. The cones of the whitebark pine are chock full of large nuts, which have a delicious, piney flavor. But a hiker will seldom have the good fortune to taste them, as the crop is harvested by the Clark's nutcrackers as fast as they ripen—or faster. The birds often can be seen working the cones in the tops of trees, systematically extracting the nuts from unripe cones with their long, sturdy bills. An unharvested cone or an uneaten nut seldom hits the ground. The nutcracker will rattle each nut inside its bill, determining by the nut's sound if it is edible. Seeds that are inedible because they are diseased or unfertilized are discarded.

How can a small flock of nutcrackers possibly harvest all the pine nuts in the forest? In one of the most remarkable behavior patterns of all Montana birds, the nutcrackers systematically cache their seed crop, burying the seeds in thousands of tiny stashes all across the mountainside.

The nutcrackers are adapted to carry a supply of seeds in special pouches beneath their tongues. In their late-summer forays, the birds fill these pouches, then fly several miles to a seed-burial site, usually located on a bare, south-facing slope where the snow will not be very deep the next winter. The nutcracker scrapes a hole in the soil, deposits the seeds, rakes the soil back over the cache, then places a pebble, twig or pine cone on top of the cache to camouflage it. A typical cache contains four or five seeds, and one nutcracker can hoard more than 30,000 seeds in one season. The birds rely on these seeds for their late-winter food supply—and in fact the seeds allow them to begin nesting as early as February, long before most other bird species.

But the most remarkable aspect of this behavior is the birds' ability to find their seed hoards—thousands and thousands of them, scattered across a mountainside. How do they do it? How can they remember the precise location of these individual caches so well that they can return to them months later when much of the ground is covered with snow?

Biologists Stephen Vander Wall, Diana Tomback and Russell Balda have conducted extensive investigations of the nutcracker's seed-hoarding behavior to answer these questions. These researchers studied birds penned in aviaries and allowed them to cache seeds on a sandy floor where large rocks were arranged in a systematic pattern. They later moved some of the rocks eight inches in one direction, but kept the same pattern. When the birds returned to find their caches, they would dig in the wrong spot: eight inches from the real cache in the same direction as the stones had been moved. This indicates that the birds remembered the cache locations by memorizing their position in respect to adjacent landmarks, such as rocks, trees, logs and shrubs.

The nutcrackers recover most of the buried seeds, but not all. They often cache two or three times as many seeds as they possibly can use, and some seeds survive to germinate in the spring. Thus, the nutcrackers help the tree species colonize new areas. Biologist Philip Wells has estimated that the heavy seeds of pines would normally disperse only about 100 yards a year under the most favorable conditions. With the aid of nutcrackers, they are able to disperse many miles each year. This is probably the mechanism whereby many of the unexpected, high-mountain conifer species like whitebark pine made their way to such remote outliers as the Sweetgrass Hills toward the close of the last glacial epoch, when much of central Montana was forested.

scattered islands of various sizes distributed throughout the grassland sea at varying distances from the "mainland" of the Rocky Mountains. Most of these isolated ranges, like the Sweetgrass Hills, Little Rockies and Bearpaw Mountains, are volcanic in origin. They are laccoliths, or congealed blisters of molten rock that pushed up through the layers of sediment that made up the Great Plains sometime during the Tertiary. They have therefore been around for millions upon millions of years.

As montane habitat islands, however, the islands of the plains have not been around for a long time. As recently as 50,000 years ago, the Sweetgrass Hills were surrounded entirely by glacial ice a thousand feet thick. Moving south out of Canada, the ice pushed up against the northern edges of the Highwood and Bearpaw mountains. As recently as 13,000 years ago, glaciers still were advancing into the Northern Plains—though not nearly as far south—and both climate and vegetation were very different from what they are today. Thus, although the island mountains themselves are very old, the plant and animal communities have not been around long enough to develop any striking new forms of life—like Charles Darwin's finches of the Galapagos Islands or the honeycreepers of Hawaii.

So I should not have expected to find new and unique species on these montane islands. But there were still some hard questions to be answered. How many and what kinds of species have successfully survived on the islands of the plains? How are their numbers related to the equilibrium theory and to island size and degree of iso-

lation? The answers to these questions depend on which group of species you consider and are surprisingly different for plants, birds and mammals. The following is a summary of how the distribution patterns of these three groups of species differ in this unique inland island system.

Plants

The first surprises come when we consider the species of plants found on the montane islands. It is true

that many interesting relict species are found, survivors of an environment that has changed considerably since their arrival. These are usually arctic-alpine species or boreal species normally found much farther north. For example, a small patch of meadow sorrel, an arctic-alpine species, is found on the summits of the Sweetgrass Hills, and bare-stemmed mitrewort and high-bush cranberry, both boreal species,

Conifers such as this limber pine are not as likely to spread from mountain to mountain by seed dispersal as are plants that can propagate by air- or animal-borne seeds. LARRY THOMPSON

have been found in the Bearpaw Mountains.

But aside from these surprising relicts, most of the island range species of grasses and wildflowers are much the same as those found in similar habitats in the Rocky Mountains east of the Continental Divide. This is largely because the "grassland sea" is not an effective barrier to dispersal for most of these species. Seeds are readily carried to the islands from the Rockies by the prevailing westerly winds, in the droppings of migrating birds or on the fur of wide-ranging predators such as the coyote and, at one time, the wolf. A constant "rain" of potential plant colonists falls on these islands from distant sources. The differences in species composition are therefore due more to habitat differences than to the degree of isolation.

But the story is quite different in the case of coniferous trees. Conifers are evergreen or cone-bearing trees such as pines and firs. In Montana east of the Divide, the montane conifers— that is, those largely restricted to mountainous habitats— are Douglas fir, whitebark pine, lodgepole pine, limber pine, subalpine fir and spruce. (Most central Montana spruce are actually hybrids of two species, white spruce and Engelmann spruce.) Two other conifer species, ponderosa pine and Rocky Mountain juniper, are common in low-elevation, non-mountainous habitats between the montane islands. Unlike grasses and wildflowers, the montane conifer species have heavy, bulky cones and seeds that are not likely to be carried across the grassland sea by wind or mammals, although birds like the Clark's nutcracker may be important in this task. We would

therefore expect that the smaller, most isolated islands would have only one or a few species, and that only the largest islands would harbor all species.

With the difficulties inherent in the transportation of the bulky conifer seeds, it is quite remarkable to find a healthy variety of evergreens in all of the mountain islands, regardless of their size or degree of isolation. Tiny East Butte in the Sweetgrass Hills, 90 miles from the nearest seed source on the Rocky Mountain Front and with a forested area of only five square miles, harbors *all* of the species of montane conifers found in the Little Belts, which cover an area of nearly 1,500 square miles and are separated from the Continental Divide mainland by only a few miles of open grassland. Contrary to the equilibrium theory, it appears that size and distance from the mainland make little difference in determining the number of species.

Geologic history explains the unexpected presence of these species in the smallest of the island ranges. At the close of the last great glacial epoch (12,000 to 20,000 years ago), the climate of central Montana was probably sufficiently cool and moist to support conifers across the northern prairies, where they could not possibly survive today. The entire area may not have been covered by vast sweeping forests as are found today in northern Alberta and Saskatchewan, but pockets of montane conifers likely survived in steep river breaks, escarpments and badlands scattered throughout the prairie.

As the climate became warmer and drier, grasslands vigorously reinvaded the prairies, and the montane conifers were forced to retreat to the

Mountain Goat

In the highest, dizziest crags of the tallest, steepest mountain islands lives an alpine paradox, the goat that is not a goat, the native that is not a native, the animal that biologist Douglas Chadwick has called "the beast the color of winter"— the mountain goat.

This shaggy, ghost-white creature is one of the few truly alpine mammals found in Montana. It is not strictly a goat, but rather is a goat-antelope, more closely related to the chamois of the Alps.

Mountain goats are unusual animals in many respects. Unlike most large ungulates— such as elk, deer and bighorn sheep, whose adult males dominate the social structure— mountain goat societies are dominated by adult females.

Adult males behave as subordinates and stay out of the way of the other classes most of the time. When courting females during the rut, they crawl on their bellies and make soft squeaking sounds like a kid. After mating, the billy is chased away by the dominant nanny.

Goats also have some remarkable adaptations to life in their severe alpine habitat. They have compact, muscular bodies flattened from side to side for greater balance on narrow ridges and ledges. Their hooves give maximum traction on steep rock ledges. And their shaggy pelage, consisting of long, hollow guard hairs and short, dense wool, is an effective insu-

Opposite page: The mountain goat's seeming placidity may be a protective behavior that prevents unnecessarily dangerous reactions in its lofty home.
TOM ULRICH
Left: Nannies often bear two young, but the mortality rate in many years is at least 50 percent.
ED WOLFF

lation even when wind-chill factors exceed 70 below zero, as they often do at high elevations during Montana winters.

Mountain goats are native to Montana, but only to the alpine peaks of the western part of the state. The broad intermountain grasslands of central Montana were a highly effective barrier to their dispersal, and goats never were able to naturally colonize the isolated montane islands of central Montana. Thus, they were historically absent from these isolated ranges. An exception could be the Pryors, where naturalist Charles E. McChesney reported a herd of 15 or 20 in 1878.

In 1941, however, the Montana Department of Fish and Game (now Fish, Wildlife and Parks) began a program to introduce goats into these islands of suitable but vacant habitat. The first coordinated transplant of 21 animals was made in the Crazy Mountains along Sweetgrass Creek in 1941 and 1943. The transplant was made at the request of local rancher Barney Brannin, who raised half the funding for the project from local residents and who helped the game managers trap the animals from the Deep Creek area west of Choteau.

Over the next quarter century other successful transplants were made into the Absaroka-Beartooths, Square Butte east of the Highwood Mountains and the Big Snowy Mountains. Goats now are established in most of the state's suitable habitat, but they are not native to the island ranges they now occupy.

Probably the most astonishing success was the Crazy Mountains transplant. In 1953, ten years after the first goats found a home there, the first hunting season was opened when the goat population probably numbered around 275. The population continued to boom. By 1955, the population had grown to a peak of 325 or more. Goats swarmed over every ridge and crag of the Crazies, in such numbers that every sprig of vegetation was chewed.

But the boom was short-lived. In 1957, 120 of an estimated 315 goats were harvested, and shortly afterwards the population crashed. By 1961 the population had decreased to 160, and by 1970 it was down to 62 goats. The last hunting season on goats in the Crazies was in 1976. Since then the population has fluctuated between 35 and 50 animals, never again approaching that of the boom years of the 1950s. This pattern is typical of animals introduced to new, previously unoccupied habitats—the population initially takes off, soars to peak numbers, then crashes, never again approaching the initial peak. For example, when Himalayan thar (a goat-like animal related to the mountain goat) were introduced into the mountains of New Zealand —like the Crazy Mountains, an ecological island—a similar boom-and-bust cycle occurred.

Biologists now believe the crash of the Crazy Mountain herds was the result of damage to the fragile alpine plants caused by the initial irruption of the herd. The range had existed for millenia without goats, and suddenly, over a period of a decade, the peaks were overrun with goats, chewing every sprig of tundra in sight. The vegetation of the mountain range was simply not adapted to support 325 hungry goats. Now the tundra of the peaks is sparsely scattered among rockfields, in sharp contrast to the well developed tundra of the nearby Absaroka-Beartooth range.

Was it a mistake to allow the harvest of 120 goats in 1957? At that time, little was known about goat biology, and biologists believed that goats would respond to heavy harvest as deer and elk do—with increased reproductive rates. As it turned out, in the Crazies the opposite occurred. As more goats were harvested and the population declined, so did reproductive rates. By 1957, the goats had already done their damage to the habitat, and a decline was inevitable. The heavy harvest only accelerated the decline. Now we can say that the heavy harvest should have occurred much earlier—say, in the late 1940s when there were fewer than 200 goats. If that had been done, chances are the range would have stayed healthy and a good annual harvest would have been maintained.

A similar set of circumstances occurred when goats were transplanted into the Square Butte area near Geraldine. The population underwent an initial boom, and soon the goats were so numerous that local farmers and ranchers actually were finding goats in the open prairies surrounding the butte. Then the population crashed and has been restored only through additional transplants.

Continental glaciation, which reached some of the more northerly ranges, influenced topography and emphasized the distance between many highland features. This is country between the buttes in the Sweetgrass Hills showing potholes typical of glaciated areas where lingering ice left depressions. They still are visible today when snow accumulates in them. LARRY THOMPSON

mountain islands, the only remaining suitable habitat. It is probable that all the montane species invaded all the montane islands (with the probable exception of the Little Rockies and the Cypress Hills). In some areas, like the Sweetgrass Hills, all survive there today. In other ranges, fire, disease or drought wiped out one or more species, and today they are short of a full complement. Once the grassland sea became established, colonization ceased and extinctions began. Thus, in this case, the number of species is clearly not the equilibrium predicted by island biogeographic theory.

Mammals

Montane mammals are a group of species for which we would expect to see more of a true equilibrium effect— especially in the case of the smaller mountain- or tree-loving species. To these species, the prairie sea should easily be as effective an inter-island barrier as an ocean of water. In this part of Montana, a relatively small number of species is in this category— the montane shrew, water shrew, pika, snowshoe hare, yellow-pine chipmunk, golden-mantled ground squirrel, tree squirrel, northern flying squirrel, heather vole, water vole, montane vole, Gapper's red-backed vole and ermine. Mammals like the marten, fisher and

wolverine prefer the mountains but have large home ranges and are known to be wide-ranging; the grassland sea is not as effective a barrier to their movements.

In fact, the smaller, more isolated ranges support the fewest species of montane mammals, as we would expect. The montane shrew is the only strictly montane species found in all of the mountain islands of central Montana, while the pika is found only in the largest ranges— the Little Belts, Crazies and Bighorns. These ranges and the Snowy Mountains, another big range, support the most montane species— as many as nine per range. In contrast, the smallest ranges, such as the Little Rockies

and Sweetgrass Hills, offer homes to only one or two species.

This looks suspiciously like a true equilibrium situation— until we consider the history of the ranges. Fifteen thousand years ago, when coniferous forests covered much of the central Montana prairie, the mammals had easy access to the mountain islands. As the prairie dried and the islands were separated by grasslands, immigration stopped and extinctions began to take their toll, one species at a time. For instance, it is very likely that tree squirrels once were present in the Sweetgrass Hills, but were wiped out by forest fires, disease or some other evolutionary cataclysm. The

Some people are surprised to learn that the mountains of eastern Montana harbor good elk populations, but the elk are there nonetheless, giving the mountain islands a special wild quality.
Above: Two bulls engage in a spring sparring match. MICHAEL QUINTON
Right: Elk enjoys the relatively stress-free days of summer. JAN WASSINK

Elk

The elk, an animal we so closely associate with mountains, was once a prairie animal that ranged throughout eastern Montana. Prince Maximilian, an early visitor to the upper Missouri country, described (1833) a pyramid of elk antlers that had been erected by the Indians near present-day Wolf Point. It stood 16 to 18 feet high and 12 to 15 feet in diameter. Pushed into different habitat by the pressures of civilization, elk now are largely restricted to forested, mountainous areas where timber cover and terrain give the security that the valleys and plains no longer can provide.

Healthy elk populations now exist in the Sweetgrass Hills, Bearpaws, Highwoods, Judiths, Little Belts, Snowies, Crazies and Castles. They are also found in the Bull Mountains south of Roundup and in the Missouri Breaks as far downstream as Wolf Point.

My first view of the East Butte elk herd in the Sweetgrass Hills is one I am not likely to forget. I had been climbing through the woods toward the high saddle that separated Mount Brown and Mount Royal, carrying a pack heavy with supplies and specimen-collecting gear. When I arrived at the saddle, I threw my load on the ground and collapsed beside it. Then I looked up for the first time— to see a herd of 20 or more elk not more than 100 feet away! The population has grown steadily and significantly, and biologists now estimate the size of the Sweetgrass Hills herd at more than 200 head. In recent years 50 permits annually have been issued for the area, and 20 to 35 elk are harvested each year.

Elk in central Montana are strongly migratory. In summer they inhabit high, moist timbered habitats in the more remote reaches of the island ranges. During the fall rut, the mountains ring with the musical bugling of the bulls. When the heavy snows of late fall begin, elk move downslope to windswept, grassy south-facing slopes, where lesser snow depths allow them to reach and eat bunchgrasses. In spring they move back to the high country. Cows usually drop their calves in late May or early June in habitats just above the upper limits of the winter range.

Although Maximilian's elk-horn pyramid is gone forever, today's visitors to eastern Montana's island mountains have a good chance of viewing these mountain monarchs.

Rich texture of green is a forest of subalpine fir in the Sweetgrass Hills.
LARRY THOMPSON

Subalpine Fir

One of the most unexpected species in the island mountains is subalpine fir, a tree species of the high, moist forests near timberline in the main ranges of the Rockies. Subalpine fir is one of the most beautiful of the conifer species, usually taking the tall, narrow form of a cathedral spire. Its needles resemble those of the Douglas fir but tend to sweep upward on the branches. Also, subalpine fir has rounded buds at the ends of the branches, while Douglas fir has pointed buds. The cones of subalpine fir project upward from the branches and disintegrate while still on the tree, so that cones are seldom found beneath the tree. The cones of Douglas fir, on the other hand, hang downward, fall intact and accumulate beneath the tree.

Subalpine fir can survive only where conditions are sufficiently cool and moist. In the Sweetgrass Hills, for example, it is found on the summits of Mount Royal and West Butte at an elevation just under 7,000 feet. In this severe, wind-swept environment, the trees take on an unusual form. They are often surrounded by shrubby "skirts" extending several yards around the base of each tree, and some trees take on the appearance of "krummholz" — the twisted, gnarled, shrub-like trees found at timberline. But subalpine fir also is found at the relatively low elevation of 5,500 feet in upper Ribbon Gulch on East Butte. Here it grows beside Douglas fir and lodgepole pine in the bottom of the gulch and assumes the typical spire-like shape. It is able to survive here because of cold-air drainage; the colder, heavier air flows down the slope at night filling the gulch and making the environment sufficiently cool and moist for the trees to survive.

grassland barrier is so effective in preventing movement of these species that colonization has virtually stopped. So, small-mammal species numbers, like those of conifers, are not in equilibrium in this inland archipelago. They will do nothing but decrease over time.

Big-game mammals are a different story altogether. Before white settlement times, species such as the grizzly bear, elk and bighorn sheep ranged freely across the lowland habitats between the island ranges. But man's development activities — settling, sodbusting, road-building— have strengthened the barriers between the island mountains. Most populations of these species have been wiped out from the plains habitats that separate the islands, and these environments have become much less hospitable to the animals

Dr. Harold Picton of Montana State University has been studying distributions of big-game animals on these montane islands and has arrived at the following conclusion: Prior to settlement, the island mountains of central Montana were much less island-like than they are today. The insularity of the mountain islands was increased by agriculture, roads, and subsistence hunting. Many species became extinct on the smaller mountain ranges as a result of these pressures. The wildlife-restoration program begun by the state Department of Fish and Game in the 1940s, however, not only was successful in restoring many of the lost populations— especially in the larger ranges— but also it succeeded in establishing new populations in historically vacant habitat. These changes have to some degree ameliorated the effects of development on species distribution patterns. Dr.

Picton also found that the number of large-mammal species now occurring on the montane islands tends to increase both with island area and with the topographic diversity of the island.

Birds

Birds are an exceptionally diverse group in Montana. Certainly, more than a hundred breeding species can be found in just about every county in the state. For most of them, a hundred miles of grassland is hardly a barrier at all. In fact, many species migrate thousands of miles every spring and fall. Some species, like the pileated woodpecker, though able to fly great distances, prefer to be stay-at-homes. Others, particularly mountain grouse, seldom fly more than a few hundred yards at a time and can be considered as sedentary as some montane mammals. Birds, then, are not a simple group to analyze in terms of island biogeography.

It is not surprising to learn that all of central Montana's mountain islands harbor a diversity of migratory birds. A standard group of montane species (that is, species largely restricted to forested, mountainous habitats) is found in nearly every isolated range: the dusky flycatcher, Clark's nutcracker, mountain chickadee, ruby-crowned kinglet, red-breasted nuthatch, Swainson's thrush, Townsend's solitaire, yellow-rumped warbler, western tanager, pine siskin, red crossbill and dark-eyed junco.

The number of species of strictly montane birds shows some relation to the size of the mountain area. The smaller ranges (Sweetgrass Hills, Bearpaws, Little Rockies and Judiths) harbor from 15 to 19 breeding species of truly montane birds. The

Pryor, Snowy and Highwood mountains are home to from 23 to 25 species, and the massive Little Belt range has no fewer than 37 species of mountain-loving birds. If the dry prairie presents no real barrier to the passage of these migratory birds, why do not all species occur in all the ranges? Part of the answer, as with plants, lies in the types of habitat offered by the various mountain islands. Larger islands as a rule support a greater diversity of habitats—moist canyons, old-growth forests, springs, good-sized streams, stands of shrubs and willows. Consequently, species like the Steller's jay, calliope hummingbird, three-toed woodpecker, dipper and Lincoln's sparrow—all of which prefer the dense, lush forests common to western Montana—can find a suitable home in the Little Belt Mountains but would not thrive in the dry forest of the Sweetgrass Hills.

The absence of some species, however, cannot be entirely attributed to lack of suitable habitat. For instance, white-crowned sparrows are found in the nearby Cypress Hills of Canada but not in the similar habitat of the Sweetgrass Hills. The pine grosbeak lives in the Sweetgrass Hills but not in the much larger Highwoods to the southeast. Chance has a role in the explanation. The patches of suitable habitat on these smaller islands are so small, they may simply be missed by migrating birds during some years. Or, they may be colonized only to have disease or predation wipe out both parents and progeny in certain bad years. The particular community of birds breeding on any one of the montane islands may therefore differ from year to year.

Over the long term, however, I have

Above: Versatile and cunning, the bobcat frequents many eastern Montana mountain ranges. ALAN CAREY
Above right: Perhaps the most persevering predator of them all is the coyote. TIM CHRISTIE
Right: Goldfinch in sunflowers, not an uncommon sight in our island mountains. CRAIG AND LIZ LARCOM
Far right: Marten tracks. MICHAEL QUINTON

found that bird communities on the montane islands are surprisingly stable. In 1983, 10 years after my first field investigation in the Sweetgrass Hills, I walked exactly the same routes at the same times of day to see the changes of a decade. I was amazed to find how similar the bird populations were. A dusky flycatcher was occupying the same territory occupied by its great-great-great-grandpappy 10 years before. Western tanagers still sang from the same branch of the same tree. I found the merlin nest I had sought 10 years earlier, in the same grove of trees where I once had searched. I

Mule deer buck. MICHAEL QUINTON

Mule Deer

The mule deer is the most ubiquitous of Montana's big-game animals. Just about every township in the state has a mule deer population. Thus, it is not surprising that mule deer are the most abundant big-game animal in most of the mountain islands.

Unlike elk and mountain sheep, which are primarily grazing animals, mule deer are browsers, subsisting primarily on shrubby vegetation supplemented in the summer by tender forbs. Consequently, in the island mountain ranges they are not animals of dense, continuous stands of timber but prefer open habitats adjacent to timber cover— places where browse species such as chokecherry and serviceberry are abundant. The sterile lodgepole pine forests that cloak north-facing slopes in many of the island ranges do not support much in the way of forage and are not good deer habitat.

Deer, like elk and bighorn sheep, migrate to traditional winter ranges at lower elevations with the first heavy snows of fall. These ranges are often windswept, south-facing slopes, especially in areas where big sagebrush, a favorite winter forage species, is plentiful. When the higher elevations of the montane islands are buried under the snow, wintering herds of mule deer move to the lower foothills and onto the surrounding prairie.

Studies of mule deer in the montane islands have revealed some unique aspects— for example, population numbers and reproductive rates seem to be more stable than they are in the surrounding prairie habitats. But for the most part, mule deer in the mountain islands are as they are everywhere in the state— widespread, adaptable and thoroughly enjoyable to see.

found no new montane species and missed only three I had spotted in 1973, which was not surprising, since I spent much less time in the area on my second trip. The species that were common in 1973 were still common and in about the same relative proportions.

To me, the island mountain ranges give the impression of very low diversity and abundance, when compared with "mainland" habitats. In these ranges I could walk for many minutes without encountering a bird of any species, something that just does not happen in the teeming montane forests of the main Rockies of western Montana. It seems that vacant habitat is just begging for wildlife— silent rockfalls without pikas or golden-mantled ground squirrels, meadows without white-crowned sparrows, conifer groves without Cassin's finches, streambanks without frogs, snakes or rodents. A true desert isle.

Perhaps this is why some species are inexplicably absent from the smaller ranges. The habitat is marginal. It is only visited by a few birds each spring. It is off the beaten path. Migrating birds may pass it by in hopes of finding something better down the line.

Conclusions

So none of the plants, the birds, or the mammals of the islands of the Plains is in a true equilibrium between immigrations and extinctions. Does this mean the equilibrium theory is not valid in this situation, or that the montane outliers are not true islands? On the contrary, these are the exceptions that prove the rule, and these unexpected results support the theory as much as island systems that conform perfectly to theoretical predictions. And let there be no question: these mountain outliers are truly ecological islands--as much so as tropical isles in the Pacific Ocean.

The islands of the Plains are a living laboratory in which to study some of the big questions of ecology: why species are where they are and in the numbers they are. In these quiet, lonely outposts, the many small dramas of animal populations are played out largely unnoticed by man. I found no new species in the islands of the Plains, no bizarre Mesozoic relicts or evolutionary aberrations. But I certainly was not disappointed. None of the species groups I studied conformed precisely to the equilibrium theory. This finding in itself adds to our understanding of the patterns that control animal distribution and abundance. My snapshot view of this dynamic, ever-changing living community was to me more exciting than the most gripping science fiction— for it provided a glimpse of a few frames of a long-hidden movie.

Pink pincushion cactus. KRISTI DuBOIS

Mountain Sheep

Rocky Mountain bighorn sheep. ED WOLFF

The breaks, badlands and island mountains of central Montana were once the home of the now extinct subspecies of mountain sheep, *Ovis canadensis audubonii*, or Audubon's bighorn sheep. These animals were nearly identical to the race of Rocky Mountain bighorns that inhabits western Montana today, differing in habitat and diet, in the heaviness of the jaw and the shape of certain skull bones.

As grazing animals, mountain sheep require habitat with steep escape terrain adjacent to lush meadows of bunchgrasses. Escape terrain can be provided either by steep mountain cliffs or by the abrupt breaks and badlands along major river valleys, places where the sheep can escape predation by large carnivores— in former times, principally the gray wolf. They descend to the grasslands in winter to feed but seldom stray

more than a hundred yards or so from the safety of the cliffs. Prior to white settlement, Audubon's bighorns were distributed widely throughout eastern Montana, North and South Dakota and Wyoming, inhabiting breaks and badlands along the lower Missouri and Yellowstone rivers as well as the island mountain ranges such as the Sweetgrass Hills and Bearpaw Mountains.

The extinction of the race followed inevitably upon the heels of the early settlers, traders and stockmen. The animals were easy prey for riflemen shooting from riverboats, because the sheep found what they may have thought to be security atop the inaccessible knobs and pinnacles. But disease was probably the most important factor in the demise of Audubon's bighorns. The sheep were abundant in the Bearpaw Mountains as

late as 1885 but were gone by 1897 because of anthrax contracted from domestic sheep.

It is not known when the last Audubon's bighorn passed from the scene; small herds probably hung on in remote places like the Sweetgrass Hills as late as the 1920s. According to biologist Faye M. Couey, writing in 1950, "Bighorns were once plentiful in the Crazy Mountains but the last ones disappeared in the late 1920s. The same is true of the Snowy Mountains, Judith Mountains, Pryor Mountains, Little Rocky Mountains and the Bear Paw Mountains. In the Big Belt Mountains sheep were once numerous, but the only ones present now are a few transplanted from the Sun River in 1943."

Mountain sheep— the western race— have been transplanted into some of the mountain islands with limited success. Herds now survive in some of the larger ranges such as the Pryors, Little Rockies and Big Belts. They are even thriving in the Sheep Mountains near Miles

City. The greatest success with transplanted herds has been in the Blue Mountains of southeastern Montana. In 1958, 11 sheep were transplanted there, followed by 25 more in 1976. This herd now has increased to more than 100 animals.

Without a doubt the most striking feature of the mountain sheep is the male's curled horns. In adult males these horns may weigh as much as the animal's entire skeleton. The first explorers to observe this unique species were hard-pressed to find a function for these enormous structures and were further confused by the fact that the male's forehead was often bloody and battered. John Palliser, who explored eastern Montana in 1847-48, believed that the heads and horns were built sturdily "as to enable the animal safely to fling himself on his head from very considerable heights." Today we know that the horns are an adaptation for the spectacular head-butting that occurs among rams during the fall rut.

hi-line mountain ranges

Blackfeet Indians—Three Buttes (Sweetgrass Hills). From U.S. Pacific Railroad Surveys. Volume 12

At the turn of the century, westbound passengers on the Great Northern Railway knew they were nearly halfway across the immense prairie when they gained a clear view of the Little Rocky and Bearpaw mountains to the south. As the train skirted the west end of the Bearpaws, travelers then noticed the faint blue outline of the Sweetgrass Hills far to the north.

These mountains were frontier signposts, landmarks that suddenly gave dimension, relief and a sense of destination to the seemingly interminable horizon. Their distinctiveness evoked a sense of imminent change, an anticipation of new landscapes and a premonition of the great land barrier, the Rocky Mountains.

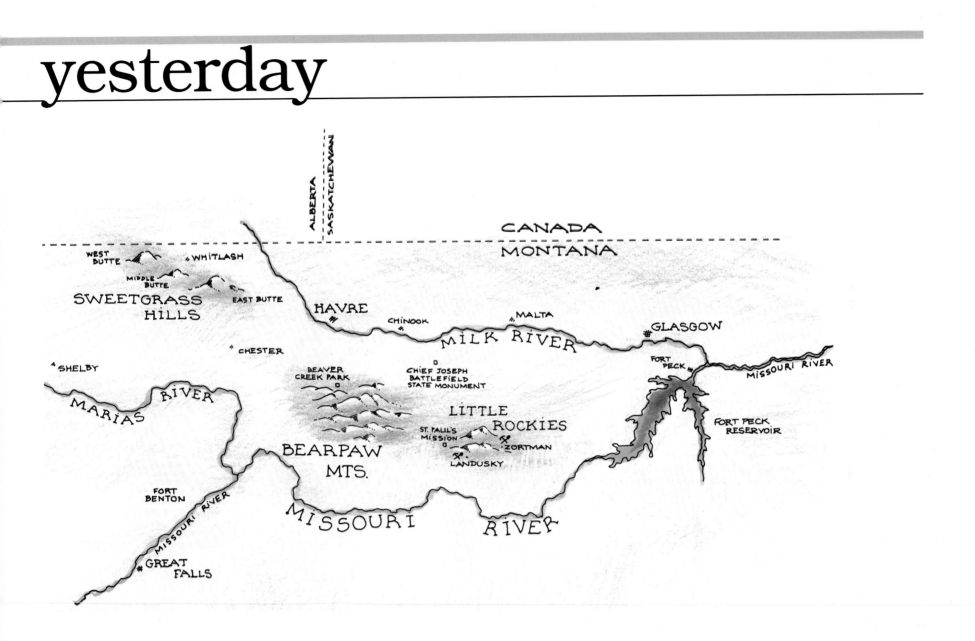

The Great Northern, built across northern Montana in 1887, gave the splendid high prairie its popular name— the Hi-Line. Along that mainline were communities whose immigrants longed to recreate new versions of the old country in towns like Glasgow, Malta, Zurich and Havre.

The Hi-Line prairies have seen dramatic changes since the building of the railroad. Grain and hay crops now dominate river bottoms that were once knee-high in prairie grasses. Cows and sheep occupy the former domain of the buffalo, and frame houses and grain elevators have replaced native tipis and the shacks of homesteaders. Less habitable and not easily tilled for agricultural gold, the mountains have remained much the same as they were a century ago.

The island mountains of the Hi-Line region lie north of the Missouri River and subdivide the basins of that river's northern tributaries. Farthest from the river, draining into the glacial plains surrounding the Marias River, the Sweetgrass Hills are a little-known slice of alpine mountains on the Montana-Canada border. A hundred miles east of the Continental Divide, their abrupt rise from acres and acres of grassland is startling. After Browning, the eastbound traveler sees nothing higher than a grain elevator on a landscape veneered by endless wheat fields. Then, suddenly, these almost conical hills appear, an island range in its purest sense. The Sweetgrass Hills are cattle, oil and wheat country and, for Blackfeet Indians, are a sacred place of spiritual renewal.

To the southeast, the low wall of the Bearpaws separates the Milk and Missouri river basins. From a great distance the mountains are a mirage of blue peaks hanging in the rippled air. Bubbling, gin-clear, up-to-your-knees, trout-filled mountain streams are rare in eastern Montana, but they flow from the broad slopes of the Bearpaws.

Closest to the Missouri itself, the Little Rockies are the sentinel of the arid badlands of the Missouri River Breaks. That great boil of igneous rock has eroded into a cluster of peaks as rugged as any found on the Continental Divide.

Upper Missouri Basin History

Early European-American settlers came to the western United States in distinct waves of migration. They settled Montana in much the same pattern as they did in other Western states: first came the explorers, followed by trappers, traders and hunters, who brought miners, who opened new pastures for cattlemen, whose ranges were finally claimed by homesteaders.

The development of Montana's Hi-Line was no exception. People seeking new lives on the frontier initially moved from east of the Mississippi River up the Missouri to join others who would harvest the unexploited natural riches of Montana. Over time, one immigrant group displaced another in competition for the resources that drew them to the territory.

A few got rich without staying to see one winter in Montana, but most returned to "the States" with less in their pockets than when they arrived. Those who remained and prospered were the ones flexible enough to adjust to the frontier's many occupational fluctuations and nature's rigorous demands. As the waves of exploitation swept across the state, the survivors were prepared to swim with them.

The people who came to the Hi-Line trapped beaver, hunted buffalo, excavated hillside mines and ran great swarms of livestock on the virgin grasslands north of the Missouri. The prairie mountains were the original signposts of those frontiers. The pioneers sought them for shelter, wood, and clean running water, and they built the first Hi-Line communities near the deposits of precious minerals they found.

As the mountains' surface minerals gave out, the communities that once thrived on them were abandoned. The terraces of the Missouri River and its tributaries then captured the permanent settlements, as agriculture, transportation and commerce came to dominate the Hi-Line economy. Though it became impractical for all but a few to live in them, the prairie mountains continued to offer their bounty— game, timber, minerals, clean water and the pleasures of mountain atmosphere.

About 30,000 years ago, the Hi-Line ranges were truly inhospitable knobs of land rising at the edge of an ice sheet a thousand feet thick. As these continental glaciers melted, Asian hunters followed herds of bison, wooly mammoth (an arctic species of elephant) and

Our eastern mountains were sentinel posts in the plains tribes' constant search for bison. TOM MURPHY

caribou across a land bridge into North America.

The descendants of these prehistoric hunters established the Great North Trail, from Alaska through central Montana, into Mexico. Their stone tools have been found in the foothills of the prairie mountains. Around 4,000 years ago, they disappeared, probably migrating to a moister environment.

Of the native tribes first encountered by whites, only the Flatheads and Nez Perces, who lived west of the Rockies, had hunted the eastern Montana prairie before 1600. Other tribes were "new" to the region, pushed westward like marbles in a tube as Europeans took Indian land on the eastern seaboard and inland woodlands.

By 1750 the Blackfeet had asserted their dominance over the vast plains north of Montana's Missouri River. Like most Plains Indian groups, they adapted to the environment of the prairie and skillfully harvested its bounty—the buffalo. The horse, introduced by Spaniards in New Mexico around 1680 and traded to the Blackfeet early in the 18th century, and the gun, further enhanced their nomadic hunting lifestyle.

These people lived year-round in tipis made from hides strung around poles procured from the prairie mountains. Their provisions and gear were carried by travois—poles crossed over the back of a horse or dog at one end, a loaded platform on the other. Tipi and travois, hallmarks of this mobile hunting culture, thus required materials available in the hills above the prairie.

The success of the hunt depended not only on the hunter's skill and preparation, but also on the rituals that appeased the many spirits of native cosmology. Men often would go to the mountains to fast and gain visions from the spiritual world—a rite of passage for the young, a ritual of guidance and renewal for older leaders. The mountains offered the vision seekers elevation—physically and spiritually lifting them above ordinary existence.

Katoysix, the Blackfeet word for the Sweetgrass Hills, literally means "place of the sweet pine." The Indians burned "sweet pine," or Douglas fir for incense in ceremonies. It also had medicinal value as a poultice for fevers and chest colds. Mixed with grease, it was used as hair tonic.

In *Death, Too, for the Heavy Runner*, Ben Bennett recreates the vision quest of a Blackfeet chief in the Sweetgrass Hills. After four days of solitary fasting and praying, high on the mountain top, the spiritual world opened to Heavy Runner and spoke to him in the form of a bird:

"'What did you see?' asked Raven.

"'I see Earth, our mother,' I answered, 'with all her sons and daughters, in all their faces.'

"'You have seen something,' said Raven. 'The ground has mercy for all. At her breast all living things, with legs or wings or fins or roots, are little children nursing.'

"'I see that all Earth's children are one with all who have been or will be,' I answered.

"'You have seen something,' said Raven. 'You have seen the sacred hoop. It is the circle of life. Everything is enclosed within it. Everything within it is the same.'

"Shadow and bird, we returned to the Sweet Grass Hills and my place of fasting. There Raven departed. I watched his dark wings, heard his powerful words."

"'Keep the sacred hoop,' he called, 'and all directions lead to home.'"

Missouri River west of Fort Benton with Highwoods in the background.
MARK MELOY

In 1870 Heavy Runner and 173 of his people were murdered when Major Eugene Baker and his troops launched an unprovoked attack on the Indians' peaceful camp along the Marias River. Major Baker allegedly was drunk when he charged the camp on that frigid January morn-

ing. He had mistakenly assumed that this was the camp of Mountain Chief, whom he sought for the murder of a white settler. Though the incident became a controversy in the nation's newspapers, the U.S. War Department exonerated Baker for his part in the massacre.

Reports held that Heavy Runner was the first to die in the slaughter, when he ran from his tipi waving some papers at the soldiers— papers that ironically declared his loyalty to the U.S. government.

Early White Explorers & Miners

Although a few intrepid non-Indian trappers entered the country before them, the first formal exploration of the land of the Blackfeet came with the Lewis and Clark expedition in 1805. Gazing at the hazy blue silhouettes afloat on a clear expanse of high plains, Captain Meriwether Lewis felt a mixture of trepidation and joy at his first sight of the Rocky Mountains (in reality, probably the Little Rockies). Lewis wrote:

". . . while I viewed these mountains I felt a secret pleasure in finding myself so near the head of the heretofore conceived boundless Missouri; but when I reflected on the difficulties which this snowey barrier would most probably throw in my way to the Pacific . . . it in some measure counterbalanced the joy..."

To the expedition, the island mountain ranges signaled great changes, a terrain that would require immense effort to explore and traverse. At the same time, their moist, rich mountain forests interrupted the plains and spurred the explorers onward, deeper into the continent's *terra incognita*.

Other than a few courageous fur traders, few whites ventured up the Missouri to the land of the Blackfeet for a half century after Lewis and Clark. Following information picked up from the handful of mountain men who went before them, another government party set out to explore the Hi-Line country. In 1853 the Stevens Survey was commissioned to chart a northern railway route to the Pacific Ocean, came up the Missouri River, proceeded overland from Fort Benton and one party of the survey climbed into the Bearpaw Mountains. A journal of that trip notes that the "Bear's Paw itself presents a rugged, grotesque appearance, and it requires no stretch of the imagination to see in it the paw of a grizzly bear, ready to spring on the plain."

Another party of the Stevens group explored the Sweetgrass Hills and found them to be "a favorite

resort of the Blackfeet, who say that Providence created these hills for the tribe to ascend and look for buffalo."

Even as the explorers began to formally survey the country, traders already were busy with the Indians, offering the goods of the "civilized" world for furs. Journals, letters and fur company account books tell the story of the traders. A letter quoted by historian William Pearle, from a trader whose post was north of the Sweetgrass Hills in Canada, shows the traders as lawless and as stripped of formality as the land that bred them:

"Dear Friend:

"My pardner Will Geary got to putting on airs and I shot him and he is dead— the potatoes are looking well.

"Yours Truly,

"Snookum Jim"

The furs went downriver from Fort Benton, which became the head of navigation on the Missouri River as soon as the first steamboat arrived there in 1859. Barely ten years later, river traffic once limited to the

Above: Miners' picnic near Landusky circa 1899.
Left: Early Landusky.
COURTESY MONTANA HISTORICAL SOCIETY

commerce of the fur trade swelled with the masses of gold seekers headed for the fabulous southwestern Montana gold strikes at Bannack (1862), Alder Gulch (1863), and Last Chance Gulch (1864).

At first the most popular route to the gold fields was overland from Omaha and Salt Lake City. Regular attacks by "hostiles" on overland routes and improved river boat travel, however, soon (by 1866) made Fort Benton the destination of half the freight brought into the new territory. It is estimated that 1,200 tons of goods landed at the Benton levee in 1865, a figure that grew tenfold by 1879.

As the southwestern Montana gold camps thrived, the Hi-Line mountains awaited the inevitable. Although a Captain Twining, in the report of the 1874 International Boundary Expedition, said that he camped in the Sweetgrass Hills for its "delicious and cold spring water" and in passing noted the existence of gold-bearing quartz in the area, his observation fell on deaf ears. Eventually, when gold fever had

and the town slipped into oblivion nearly as fast as it rose. Yet the founding of Gold Butte was a prophetic trespass on Indian land. By 1888, Blackfeet land from the Sweetgrass Hills to the Little Rockies was opened to white exploitation.

Even before the gold camps came to the Sweetgrass Hills, miners were in the Little Rockies. In 1884 "Pike" Landusky and others established the roaring gold camp of Landusky, which initially attracted 2,000 miners and held on tenuously in the 1890s, as hardrock mining took over from the played-out placer lodes.

Primarily because of its remote location, the town of Landusky became a haven for desperados, the most famous of whom were members of the Curry Gang, led by Harvey (alias Kid Curry) Logan.

Landusky was named for its founder and deputy sheriff, Pike Landusky, a rough mountain man, buffalo hunter, whiskey trader and miner. When half his jaw was torn off by an Indian's bullet, as the legend goes, he dulled the pain with whiskey until the wound healed. At a Christmas party at Jew Jake's Saloon in 1894, Landusky was killed by Kid Curry.

fortune seekers listening to even the most ephemeral rumor, the island ranges would be altered forever.

In 1885 four men made a modest strike in the Sweetgrass Hills and founded the town of Gold Butte, within what had been declared Blackfeet land in 1850. Exercising callous disregard for the treatied rights of the Indians, the U.S. government permitted a hundred men to mine the area. Nicknamed Two Bit Gulch, its prospects faded quickly,

Above: Terraces of Snake Creek north of the Bearpaws, where Chief Joseph's band fought their final battle, and, at right, a memorial to the Battle of the Bearpaws.
MARK MELOY PHOTOS.

The preeminence of the Indian in Montana was further broken by U.S. Army victories after the defeat of Lt. Col. George Armstrong Custer south of the Yellowstone in 1876. Adding to the Blackfeet demise, the buffalo, central to the native diet and culture, was systematically eliminated. As late as 1880, millions of buffalo still roamed the plains of the Hi-Line. Four years later, hunters were scouring the land for the few that remained. The final buffalo hunt of the Blackfeet reportedly occurred in the Sweetgrass Hills, when a few young men killed the last four animals in 1884.

In 1877 a band of Nez Perce Indians (from what are now north-central Idaho and northeastern Oregon) was involved in a fracas that resulted in the deaths of several settlers. To avoid reprisal, Chief Joseph gathered his band of 700 Nez Perces and their horses and led them on an exodus to Canada. For 1,300 miles through Montana they were chased, harassed and fired upon by troops sent out from the string of forts recently established across the territory.

Engaging in tactical maneuvers that won great respect among military experts, Joseph and his military tactician, Looking Glass, eluded the foot soldiers and mounted cavalry until their retreating army was on the north side of the Bear-paw Mountains, just 40 miles from the Canadian border. In what was dubbed the "Battle of the Bearpaws," Joseph was forced to surrender.

The mountain island topography of the Hi-Line played an integral part in Chief Joseph's defeat. The Indians evaded the cavalry, slipping into the central breaks of the Missouri River and proceeded through

Abandoned homestead, Sweetgrass Hills.
R.C. DOMMER

The Kid fled "the long arm of the law," eventually riding the Outlaw Trail in Utah with Butch Cassidy's Wild Bunch. In 1901 the Wild Bunch returned to the Hi-Line and robbed the Great Northern Railway, near Malta, of $80,000. Allegedly Curry and other members of the gang escaped to South America afterwards.

Indians' Losses

With the intrusions of mining and the new rough-and-tumble communities north of the Missouri, the Blackfeet were in a poor position to hold on to their vast tract of treaty land. Their strength had been significantly diminished by smallpox. Apparently blankets stowed on board a steamboat carried the disease and today some historians believe diseased blankets were intentionally planted. As the story goes, an Indian stole a blanket, and smallpox spread among the Indians like a prairie wildfire. Estimates say that the Blackfeet alone lost two-thirds of its population to the epidemic.

the gap between the Bearpaws and Little Rockies.

Soldiers from Fort Keogh on the Yellowstone River, under the command of Colonel Nelson Miles, predicted the Indians' route and moved quickly around the eastern edge of the Little Rockies to head them off. Because the Indians stopped to rest behind the guarded wall of the Bearpaws, Miles caught up and captured them, approaching from the unguarded east side of the Little Rockies.

It is ironic that a man from a non-Montana tribe would become one of Montana's most famous Indians. Inscribed on a plaque at the state park marking the Bearpaw Battlefield are the now-famous words Joseph spoke upon his surrender:

"Hear me, my chiefs. I am tired. My heart is sick and sad. From where the sun now stands I will fight no more, forever."

The Battle of the Bearpaws was the last major conflict in the Montana Indian wars.

The millions of buffalo slaughtered on Indian land north of the Missouri were quickly replaced by cattle. An 1851 treaty had guaranteed Blackfeet control of the Hi-Line, but in 1888 the government reduced that reservation by nearly 18 million acres and removed the tribe to a small reservation at the head of the Marias River. The free-roaming days of the proud Blackfeet nation were fading. The Indian people were forced to live within a small parcel of their former empire, whose boundaries were dictated not by nature or rival tribes but by the government of the white settlers. They accepted the promises of annuities in return for the land. They had no choice; the buffalo were gone.

Cattlemen running stock on the already overstocked ranges of central Montana welcomed the opportunity to cross north of the Missouri onto new range and virgin pastures. They had only to file in the nearest weekly newspaper their intent to claim and occupy certain areas of the country.

The DHS ranch, located southeast of what is now Lewistown, was one of the large open-range operations extending north of the Missouri even before the country was legally opened to stockmen in 1888. Con Price, a cowboy working for the DHS, later reflected on the richness of the plains surrounding the Sweetgrass Hills in *Memories of Old Montana.* "I have seen," he wrote, "steers so fat we could hardly drive them into the roundups..." The cattle's remarkable growth was due to the high-protein native buffalo grass found in abundance all across the northern prairie.

Life was not easy for the cowboys who herded as many as 10,000 head, protecting them from predators, occasional renegades and the fluctuations of the weather. In *Wolf Willow,* Wallace Stegner wrote a fictional account of the lives of the open-range cowboy. In one passage Stegner followed the thoughts of a young cowboy working north of the Hi-Line as he headed for evening camp:

"How much further? Up above, the sky was pure; the Northern Lights were beginning to flare and stretch. He heard his old friend the wolf hunting down the river valleys and coulees of his ordained home and speaking his wolfish mind to the indifferent stars. Lord God, how much longer? They had been in the saddle since six in the morning, had

To pay for their immensely costly transcontinental lines, railroads solicited business by promoting the development of Montana's homestead land with advertisements such as this.
COURTESY MONTANA HISTORICAL SOCIETY

eaten nothing since then. Neither horse nor rider could take much more of this. But nobody said, we can stop now. Nobody said, we'll camp here. They couldn't, obviously. Jessie had taken their bubble of shelter God knew how many more empty miles to horse camp. He thought to himself, with a qualm of panic, My God, this is desperate. What if we don't find him? What if the horse should give clear out?"

Weather ultimately devastated the open-range cattlemen in Montana. In the "Hard Winter of 1886-1887," unsheltered and without winter feed, more than half the vast herds died of exposure. Part of the damage could

not be tallied until the spring thaw, when ranches like the DHS reported only 900 spring calves born, compared to 8,000 in the previous spring.

The cattlemen who survived restocked the ranges of their former competitors and ran the large outfits with renewed but more cautious vigor. Many began haying operations for winter feed. Some, like D.B. Phillips and Angus Dunbar, released enormous herds of sheep north of the Missouri, since sheep had survived the "Hard Winter" so much better than cattle. In 1884 there were a half million sheep in Montana; in 1886 there were a million and, by 1893, nearly two and a half million.

Homesteaders Arrive

Although many stockmen adjusted their operations to the vagaries of the northern climate, the days of open-range cattle ranching were numbered. What the cattlemen believed to be their exclusive prairie riches, others were just as anxious to have. "Charlie and I started in the cattle business too late to get the full benefit of the open range," Con Price recalled in *Memories of Old Montana*. Price, with cowboy artist Charlie Russell, ran the Lazy KY Ranch in the Sweetgrass Hills. "The cattlemen were like the Indians. At one time they had everything they wanted—free range and free water —but the sheepmen soon began to squat on the watering places and it wasn't many years until they outnumbered the cattlemen."

Competition increasingly came from the outside, as homesteaders flocked to northern-tier states to set the teeth of their plows into virgin soil. "The farmers filed on every water hole in the country and they all had dogs, so the cattle didn't have a chance," Price wrote in *Memories of Old Montana* "Some of the old-timers hung on for awhile and reminded me again of the Indians, as they said the farmer couldn't last long and would starve out and the country would go back to open range. But when I saw those farmers raise fifty bushels of wheat per acre on that virgin soil I knew it was time for an ol' hoss like me to move on."

The buffalo were gone, the Indians were confined to reservations, and the stockmen were brought to bay by barbed wire. The huge windswept prairie, dotted by gentle high ridges

The wild grasslands turned to gold for a time as unseasonably good growing conditions initially treated the Hi-Line homesteaders very well. These are two Hill County homesteads, the one at top identified as DeCelle's cabin. COURTESY MONTANA HISTORICAL SOCIETY

of blue, was the ripened plum of the prototypical land developer, as the nation began to concentrate on filling its western half in accordance with the American dream.

Like other great dreamers of his time, James J. Hill was a man of vision, the "Empire Builder" who would put millions of people to work in the "wasteland" north of the Missouri and millions of dollars into his own pockets in the process. In 1887 he acquired the necessary ease-

ments to cross Montana Territory and began to build the Great Northern Railroad. In five months he had crossed the girth of Montana with his rail line.

When he began the project, the cynics of the financial world claimed that his only cargo from that depleted northern wasteland would be buffalo and cattle bones. No one with any sense would want to settle there, they said. Yet Hill maintained that, like the rest of the West, the

vast area of public domain north of the Missouri would see a family on each 160-acre tract.

By 1909 homesteaders had taken up a million acres of Montana land; in 1910 they filed on four million more. By 1922, 42 percent of the entire area of Montana, or 93 million acres, was homesteaded. The statewide production of wheat went from 258,000 acres in 1909 to 3.4 million acres in 1919. As if the prayers of the farmers were answered, Montana received an unprecedented string of wet years, and the prairie blossomed. The Hi-Line emerged as a major wheat-producing area of the world, and thousands of families prospered.

"Bob you wouldent know the town or the country either it's all grass side down now," wrote Charlie Russell to a friend. "The boosters say its better country than it ever was but it looks like hell to me I liked it better when it belonged to God it sure was his country when we knew it."

Russell could not know that drought would befall the farmers, and the land would become the hell it looked to him. Eighty percent of the acres filed on in the boom years would later be classified as range unsuitable for farming. When the wet years proved to be the exception, and the climate resumed its normal level of annual rainfall, by August 1919, 3,000 farmers were bankrupt and destitute in J.J. Hill's namesake Hill County, according to Joseph Kinsey Howard in *Montana High, Wide and Handsome*.

Between 1921 and 1925 half of the state's farmers lost their homesteads in bank foreclosures. Half again as many mortgages were foreclosed in the next five years. The area along the Hi-Line was hardest hit. In Havre, the seat of Hill County, officials found that 90 percent of the area's farmland had been seized by creditors.

"Prospering when it rained, suffering during periods of drought," wrote Paul Sharp in *Whoop-up Country*, the plains of Canada and the U.S. were "debtor economies, relying upon the largess of outside metropolitan centers and resentful of their colonial dependence."

In the early 1920s some relief from the depressed economic conditions of the Hi-Line came with the discovery of oil in the Sweetgrass Arch, a geologic formation surrounding a large area around the Sweetgrass Hills. On the oil fields between the new towns of Kevin and Sunburst, annual production went from 400,000 to six million barrels between 1923 and 1926. For the residents of Toole County, who had endured five years of drought, the oil boom was a miracle. The people of Shelby, the county seat, looked to the hills for their future and saw their town as a thriving metropolis. The main problem was getting the tiny community on the map.

In 1923 the Shelby Chamber of Commerce organized an event designed to catch the eye of the nation: a Fourth of July boxing match between the world's heavyweight champ, Jack Dempsey, and challenger Tommy Gibbons. In the unlikely location of Shelby, Montana, carpenters constructed a pineboard arena that could seat 40,000 people and the town prepared to host a $350,000-purse prize fight.

Shelby's oil tycoons felt confident that their efforts would be generously compensated. They reported a half million dollars in reserved seats three weeks before the fight and ordered 26 special trains to carry spectators from Chicago and New York. Once in Montana, they believed, these wealthy sports enthusiasts from the East would buy oil leases and line the town's pockets.

The unexpected happened. Crucial loans fell through a few days before the fight, and nationwide headlines announced that the match was off. Dempsey's manager, Jack Kearns, would not let his fighter enter the ring until another $100,000 was produced. Yet every cent Shelby had was already in the fight. The enraged townsmen forced Kearns to compromise, guaranteeing him a cut of the gate.

Even though the trains from the East had been cancelled and all roads leading to Shelby were thick with mud from unseasonable rain storms, the event drew a large crowd. Paid admissions numbered 8,000, and several thousand more fans crashed the gates. But attendance failed to match the boosters' dreams. Financially, the event was a disaster.

Kearns escaped in the dead of night, his valise loaded with most of the cash in town. Banks from Shelby to Great Falls closed, and the town went bankrupt for several years.

The fight itself was lackluster. Gibbons survived 15 rounds but lost the fight. John K. Hutchens was then a young reporter covering the fight. In his book *One Man's Montana*, he wrote: "Who would have bet a single silver cartwheel, a year before, that Jack Dempsey would be putting his title on the line before an audience that included a former Mrs. Vanderbilt and a hundred Blackfoot Indians cheering somewhat ominously for Tommy Gibbons, a sort of hometown boy?" Gibbons' home was St. Paul, Minnesota. He had never been to Montana before and was unlikely to return.

Throughout the economic chaos, places like Shelby and Havre somehow survived and eventually prospered as the region's oil, grain and livestock resources were developed.

Far from being the obstacles that Lewis and Clark imagined, the Hi-Line mountains attracted settlers like oases on a vast desert. Indians went to them to spot buffalo and to seek prophecy on their sacred peaks. The first explorers, trappers and traders went to them for shelter and fresh spring water. Miners dug and washed precious metals in them. Cowboys sought their virgin grasses and hidden water holes. Finally, ruined homesteaders would learn, too late, that the only habitable farmland lay across the streams that flowed from the mountains. Water was the key to survival on the open prairie, and the mountains provided that essential element.

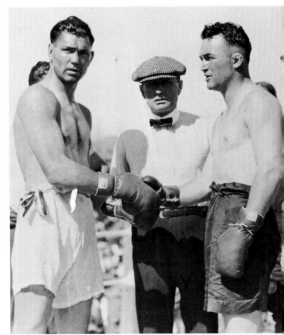

What better claim to fame for a burgeoning town like Shelby than a heavyweight boxing championship — Dempsey (left) vs. Gibbons, 1923. COURTESY MONTANA HISTORICAL SOCIETY

hi-line mountain ranges

Sweetgrass Hills

"This giant spread of land, this plain. Everywhere but to the mountained west it flowed forever," wrote A.B. Guthrie in *These Thousand Hills*, of the plains that lap the flanks of the Sweetgrass Hills. "Further than a man could think, beyond buttes blued by distance, floating in it, the earth line lipped the sky. And hardly anything, any living thing, to see . . . just emptiness and open sky. Air like tonic, days like unclaimed gold. And grass and grass and grass. Grass beyond the earth line . . . World without end."

The pyramid shapes of the Sweetgrass Hills rise from the vast stretch of prairie below them, monuments to the 49th parallel, nearly straddling the Canadian border of north-central Montana. Huge harvesters lumber toward them: camels headed for an oasis. The hills, seemingly thrown down from the heavens like lumps of

South of the Sweetgrass Hills an old house rests on an island of remnant prairie in a sea of grainfields. MARK MELOY

The Sweetgrass Hills
The Bearpaw and
The Little Rocky Mountains

mud against a wall, are the only mass to anchor the subtle, often indistinct line between sky and horizon.

Despite confusing nomenclature — they are called hills collectively and buttes individually— the Sweetgrass Hills are actually mountains, rising like errant peaks drifted 200 miles east of the Rockies. Originally called Three Buttes— Middle, West and East Butte— each is an isolated cone of igneous rock rising as separately and distinctly as the spire of a huge mountain whose base lies buried by the sediments of time.

The hills rose 50 million years ago, when a blister of molten rock broke loose from the earth's core and intruded into the sandstones of the surface. That fluid rock, or magma, hardened in cracks underground and became mountains only after eons of erosion removed the surrounding earth. Although they resemble volcanoes, there is no indication that lava ever poured onto the plains around them.

From the south the three buttes are symmetrical domes; closer examination reveals a north-trending ridgeline on each butte containing various peaks and drainages. In land area East Butte is twice as large as its sister buttes. Encompassing 30 square miles, East Butte is capped by 7,000-foot Mount Royal and flanked by alpine bowls holding the sweet odors of aspen, alder, cow parsnip and a plethora of flowers and berries. Perennial springs radiate around the butte, filling a few thin streams that run intermittently down the larger drainages ultimately to be absorbed by prairie gravels.

While grasslands are predominant on the slopes of Middle Butte, dark green mats of forest blanket East and West Buttes. These coverings of ponderosa pine, Douglas fir, lodgepole and limber pine alternate with luxuriant meadows and open talus slopes of lichen-covered boulders. The forests have seen little timber cutting and remain dense primeval thickets, dwarfed and gnarled by the cold, dry and windy climate.

The sheer dimension of the immense plain surrounding the Sweetgrass Hills truly makes them islands in a sea of grassland. The eastern front of the Rocky Mountains forms a jagged line on the western horizon, clear and distinct like a distant neighbor's picket fence. For a hundred miles south and east, the

Top: Whitlash, surrounded by the monolithic buttes of the Sweetgrass Hills, has a population between six and 22 depending on who is in town. *Left:* Elsie Demarest came to teach school in the Sweetgrass Hills 50 years ago and stayed. *Right:* Cattle rancher Claude Demarest. MARK MELOY

level plain is a quilt of strip farms abutting the low, blue Highwood and Bearpaw mountains. To the north, the Canadian plain stretches to eternity.

From atop East Butte, the 360-degree view is a flat, nearly unwrinkled landscape. Like a giant game board, the grids of black and gold strip-farms stretch across the virtually treeless plain, marked by occasional squares of shrubbery surrounding farm buildings, to dull the brunt of prairie winds.

The Sweetgrass Hills are in private ownership except for a few sections on each ridge managed by the Bureau of Land Management. Nearly all of the country immediately surrounding them also is private property, 55 percent of it cropland devoted mainly to winter wheat. Both the hills and the plains of wheat are sparsely populated, vast expanses of land against which man's measure is taken. Forty miles south of the hills is Chester, with just less than a thousand people, and about the same distance to the west is Shelby, with three times the population.

Oil and gas have contributed to the area's wheat-based economy since their discovery in the 1920s. Wells have produced in 14 different areas in and around the hills, all from the oil-rich Sweetgrass Arch, thought to be one of the largest formations of petroleum-bearing rock in the state.

Whitlash, population between six and 22 depending on who is in town on a given day, is the social center of the hills. Its mainstays are a church, school, post office and recreation hall. As difficult as it is to imagine a Montana town without a saloon, Whitlash is dry. Electrical transmission lines did not arrive in town until 1951, yet some residents had

electric generators powered by natural gas after the pipelines came through in 1929. Perhaps Whitlash's greatest step into the 20th century came not too many years ago when the dirt roads leading there were graveled.

Roberta Demarest, a rancher near Whitlash, claims the beautiful landscape of the hills is the area's most endearing quality, one she never takes for granted. The whims of weather and season constantly transform the view of the three isolated buttes surrounding her well-groomed farm. The landscape is always remarkable.

Elsie Demarest, Roberta's mother-in-law, is the family matriarch. She came to teach school in the 1930s and married Claude Demarest a few years later. "It was love at first sight," Elsie says of both Claude and the hills. She fell in love with the Sweetgrass country the moment she first stepped off the train at Chester and saw the three lonesome buttes in the distance.

Did she ever feel isolated living in so remote a place? "Never," is her emphatic answer. Her years as a young woman were filled with social functions. Every two weeks there was a dance at the town's community hall, with half of the people coming down from Canada. Those dances ended in the 1950s, not as a result of social change but because of matters of international security: the government cracked down on border crossings, and no one could cross after 5:00 p.m.

A lot more farms provided dancers back then. Over the years, Claude Demarest bought seven small ranches in the area, as homesteaders went broke and moved out. His sizable holdings now include some of the most beautiful land in the

Top: The patterns of strip farming, stretching south from East Butte in the Sweetgrass Hills. **Bottom:** Aspens on Mount Brown in the Sweetgrass Hills.
MARK MELOY PHOTOS

hills, often the stomping ground of some 200 elk. "I feed most of that herd, you'd think they would let me shoot one once in a while," Claude says of the lottery system that limits the elk hunting in the hills. Still he realizes he is fortunate to have that elk herd even without a taste of it.

In Whitlash traditional American values are still strong, personal integrity is still important and unannounced visitors are welcomed for lunch and a visit.

Bearpaw Mountains

Formed by a similar warping of the earth's crust and within sight a hundred miles southeast of the Sweetgrass Hills, the Bearpaws are an expanse of blue ripples across the horizon of the Hi-Line. From a distance they seem mere topographical aberrations. Close up, they are formidable, rising to an elevation of nearly 7,000 feet atop Old Baldy.

The range is an irregular, 50-mile spread of grassy buttes and timbered knolls watering a handful of circuitous streams. Plenty of roads slice up the Bearpaws, leading nowhere in particular. After a couple of beers on a rainy day at the Cleveland Bar in Cleveland, Montana, the backroads adventurer might easily end up mired in mud up to the axles in the forgotten territories of the Missouri Breaks south of the range.

The rounded peaks of the Bearpaws rise from 1,000 to 3,000 feet above the prairie. They are the axis and most prominent feature of the Hi-Line. Geographically they are sandwiched between the Rocky Boy's and the Fort Belknap Indian reservations and form the backdrop for Havre, the most populous town for 500 miles on Route 2 between the Continental Divide and North Dako-

ta. With a population slightly more than 10,000, seat of government for Hill County, Havre sits on the curving prairie just north of the range.

According to Rob Lucke, columnist for the Havre *Daily News*, a person is "putting on the dog" to call the range the "Bear's Paw"—yet that was the official name given the area by members of the Stevens Survey in 1853. When seen from a bluff near Big Sandy, the range is said to resemble a gigantic paw print.

Apart from Lucke's reports, little has ever been written about the range. Some recognition emanates from the 1877 surrender of Chief Joseph on the plains just north, a battle that marked the culmination of the Indian wars in Montana. Were

Left: View from the cliffs of West Butte in the Sweetgrass Hills. LARRY THOMPSON

Below: Western meadowlark. TOM ULRICH

it not for that event, few people outside the immediate area would know of the Bearpaws.

The Bearpaws are notable to Lucke in that life there has not changed since he can remember. The farm houses remain quaint and austere but well kept. The trees, fields, livestock look the same as they did when he was a kid. Even the mud holes in which he soaked his sneakers each spring on the opening day of fishing season persist. Without fail, the fishing is good in one hole of the creek but not the next, and he always manages to catch his fishing lure in the same branches. The playground of his youth remains the same today as it was 30 years ago—something that

few Americans his age can claim.

In the 1920s, the period of the honyockers, as Montana's early dryland farmers were called, the Bearpaws were the site of tremendous social upheaval. Several years of drought ruined homesteads too small to support families who had found new homes on the range's rocky soils. Spurred by false expectations, perpetuated by the hype of homestead pitchmen called locators, they attempted to take crops from land suited only for grazing.

The economic depression of the 1920s took its toll, ruining half the farmers across the state. In Hill County, 90 percent of the farm mortgages foreclosed, according to historian Joseph Kinsey Howard.

Bearpaw Baldy, as it is affectionately known by residents of the Hi-Line.
ROBERT BREWER

Old timers around Havre remember when every coulee in the Bearpaws was dotted with rough log homes and tarpaper shacks. Almost nothing remains of them now. An ambitious historian might locate a hole in the ground that had once been a root cellar of a farm that prospered through a few wet years. The wheat crops flourished across the rocky hills of the Bearpaws for a short time after 1911, but by 1919, 3,000 people were destitute in Hill County.

According to local legend, Hungry Hollow, a gullied wash in the Bearpaws, took its name from the times. One particularly harsh winter, a farmer died in the hollow and left a wife and large family. An undertaker arrived with a coffin to bury the farmer, but because the ground was too frozen for a proper burial, he dressed the corpse in a fine suit and set him in the coffin on the back porch of the house. When the ground thawed the undertaker returned to oversee proper interment. He found the man naked in his coffin. The woman had appropriated the corpse's clothing for her children.

Even today, times are tough for the families who held onto their land or bought out 160-acre homesteads for as little as $100 60 years ago and now make their living from irrigated hay crops and cattle. The Bearpaws are unique in that they have remained in the private sector whereas so much similar homestead land was abandoned and reverted to government ownership during the Depression.

However, 10,000 acres of public land lie along Beaver Creek for 15 miles into the Bearpaws above Havre. This land originally was claimed for mining when the Fort Assiniboine Military Reservation was abandoned in 1911. A group of Havre businessmen held the parcel for public recreation. Their trusteeship precluded homesteading the land or including it in the Rocky Boy's Indian Reservation.

In 1947 this land came under the control of Hill County, and today the Havre Chamber of Commerce promotes Beaver Creek Park as the largest county park in the nation, serving not only Havre but a vast area of northern Montana and southern Canada.

When the heat of summer becomes intense on the Hi-Line's open prairie, shady campgrounds along Beaver Creek offer cool relief, fishing, swimming and mountain atmosphere. Two reservoirs are well stocked with trout, and visitors may see whitetail and mule deer, bobcat, beaver, coyote, fox, mink, pheasant, grouse, eagle and hawk.

More likely, a weekend or holiday visitor will find enclaves of campers, as friends and relatives gather around trailers and tents in a tradition of family get-togethers dating from before the park's official creation. The land rush for the best of the grassy plots typically begins on Friday night, when sites are posted with family names on makeshift signs. The signs not only reserve the spots for the weekend, but also invite potential claim jumpers by for amiable visits.

The Rocky Boy's Indian Reservation, 100,000 acres of land on the west end of the Bearpaws, is the smallest and last Indian reservation established in Montana. Some of Montana's landless Indians, and Chippewa and Cree people from Canada and the Great Lakes region who arrived after other reservations had been created, were given a homeland when the government set aside the Rocky Boy's Reservation in 1916.

Rocky Boy's and Havre residents have maintained a winter recreation area in the mountains since 1969. The Bearpaw Ski Area might attract 100 visitors on a good day, despite the recurrent lack of snow. Whereas western Montana skiers are schussing down slopes a short time after Thanksgiving, Havre skiers often must wait until well after Christmas before the Bearpaw chair lift opens their backyard mountain range to the exhilaration of downhill skiing.

Amicably shared by townspeople and ranchers, Chippewa and Cree, campers and fishermen, the face of the land in the Bearpaws has changed little since whites discovered and settled the mountains a hundred years ago.

Little Rockies

"As the hawk soared down in a wide and lowering circle above the moving wagon, the whiskered wolfer lifted the old buffalo gun from his lap. Levering a cartridge into the breech without lifting the wooden stock from the wagon seat, Baker squeezed the trigger without aiming and took a give-a-damn shot at the high flying hawk.

"The report of the buffalo gun was cannon loud as the big hunk of cartridge lead, deadly enough to kill a buffalo, struck the hawk dead center. Feathers showered in midair as the lead slug tore the body into fragments. Bits of feathered flesh and bone drifted down on the startled posse members, who thought for a moment they were being ambushed by Kid Curry and his outlaw train robbers. They sat their horses in frozen bewilderment, eyeing the tall willow thickets along the creek banks that flanked the wagon road.

"'S'nabitch!' Baker's hard rasping voice sawed through the gun echoes. 'Ol' Betsey's seen'er best days. Aimed for the hawk's eye to shoot the head off neat and clean, and blowed the bird clean to hell!' He tossed the Winchester into the sagebrush and reached for the whiskey jug."
— Walt Coburn, *Pioneer Cattlemen in Montana*, 1968.

The Little Rocky Mountains rise like an apparition from the vast northeastern Montana plain 50 miles south of Malta. Sloping into the lonely, wild breaks of the Missouri River, they conjure a visual definition of all that is remote. As the stories tell, the Little Rockies were a sanctuary for outlaws where not even men of the law dared roam. Tales of Butch Cassidy and Kid

Clockwise from top: Bearpaw Ski Area. R. C. DOMMER
Where a Nez Perce soldier fell at the Chief Joseph Battleground, and Bearpaws homestead. MARK MELOY
Beaver Creek Lake in the Bearpaws. CHUCK JONES

East from Bearpaw Baldy, a gentle blend of prairie and forest. MARK MELOY

Curry are as numerous as prairie-dog holes around the mountains.

The Little Rockies form the last high clump of timbered slopes before the landscape dissolves into the northeastern Montana prairie. They include the highest eastern promontories between the Missouri River and its longest northern tributary, the Milk River. The handful of 4,000- to 6,000-foot domes are corralled into a tight cluster in a southern corner of Montana's second largest county. The land area of Phillips County is larger than Connecticut, yet has only an average of one resident per square mile.

The Assiniboine and Gros Ventre Indians gave up the southern portion of the Little Rockies to the U.S. government in 1888, an action the tribes later contested. Proceedings to repossess the land for the Indians have been ongoing since 1935. Today the Fort Belknap Indian Reservation abuts the range's north

end, while the U.S. Bureau of Land Management controls its bulk, about 25,000 acres.

Formed by the intrusion of a 10-mile-wide blister of molten syenite rock, the range is rimmed by steep, rough limestone cliffs. That rim is honeycombed by caverns that are occasionally penetrated by bold spelunkers. Many of the caves are closed to the public to protect bat hibernaculums and to preserve early Indian pictographs. One cave was dubbed Burned Man Cave in 1936, when all but 7,000 acres of the range was consumed by fire. Three men caught by the fire ducked into the cave as a last bid for survival, only to be baked and suffocated by the heat of the inferno.

The catastrophic fire burned a mature forest of ponderosa pine and Douglas fir. Thick stands of lodgepole pine, whose trunks now average five inches in diameter, have reforested the range. Some of the larger

trees of the old forest survived the fire in narrow limestone canyons, which drain the range's larger creeks. As the creeks cut across the alluvial fans at the base of the range, patches of quaking aspen and willows line the curving channels. These trees display a profusion of color around the base of the circular mountain range for a short time each autumn.

According to writer Ralph Shane, in his historical maps of the area, the Indians named the Little Rockies "the island mountains." At least one of them, Eagle Child Peak, was sacred to the Gros Ventres, who sought visions on its summit. Shane wrote, "No one ever sustained a four-night pilgrimage on Eagle Child peak. Terrifying experiences of visions of giant serpents and giant animals harass them at night about the end of the third day. Probably hallucinations from fasting."

Cowboy artist Charles Russell spent some time in the Little Rockies around 1916. A story he heard from Wallace Coburn of the Circle C ranch inspired one of his

paintings, "Loops and Swift Horses Are Swifter than Lead," in which he depicted the hog-tying of a grizzly bear with the Little Rockies as background.

In 1917, Myrtle Burke (now of Glasgow), heard the story that inspired Russell, told her by Ray Campbell, cook for the Square roundup crew that day in June 1904. She recounted the tale in *A Squawl of Wind*, the publication of the Valley County Lewis and Clark Trail Society, in 1979:

"The Square roundup crew was camped at the heads of Larb Creek and Timer Creek in present Valley County. . . . it had rained most of the night and at daybreak the nighthawk rode into camp and reported that something had spooked the horses and about 40 head were missing.

"[Bill] Jaycox [wagon boss] sent out several riders to find them. In the meantime he and a couple others rode to the top of a nearby hill. From here they spotted the horses coming at breakneck speed across the flat. . . . They then saw the

The town of Zortman in 1975. ROBERT BREWER

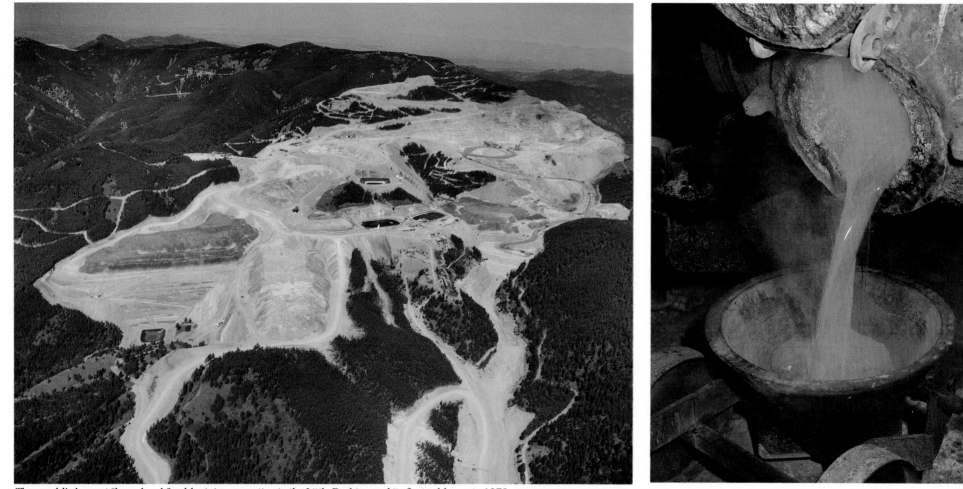

The world's largest "heap leach" gold mining operation in the Little Rockies and its first gold pour in 1979. COURTESY PEGASUS MINING COMPANY

problem: a huge brown bear was lumbering after the horses.

"[Charles] Shufelt, riding a big bronc, got in close enough to drop a loop on the bear while it was charging another rider. The bear turned and as Shufelt's horse lunged to get away the bear made a swipe with its powerful paw and tore off almost all of the horse's tail. In the meantime [Joe] Reynolds [of the Long X] and [Frank] Howe threw several loops over the bear's head, and each time the bear threw it off. Finally Reynolds got his rope on a hind foot, enabling Howe to get one over the bear's head. The well trained roping horses held the furious bear tight in the ropes.

"There was not a gun in the outfit and the men had no choice but to stone the bear to death. . . .

"Campbell. . . was fascinated by the ability of Charlie Russell to paint a scene so accurately from only a verbal description. He told me that there were only two mistakes in the picture—the cowboys were painted wearing guns; and the Little Rockies which appear rather close in the picture were really farther away, instead, the Larb Hills, just a few miles to the south, should have been in the picture."

The adventures of cowboys, Indians and outlaws may have been the fodder of local legend, but mining was the less glamorous mainstay in the Little Rockies. The discovery of gold in 1884 gave birth to the towns of Zortman and Landusky. The placer-mining boom was shortlived; hundreds came, but within months only a few remained. A scarcity of water in gulches where the gold was found made prospecting difficult. But in 1893 the miners returned to develop hardrock mines and follow

The Little Rockies as seen from the road to the Missouri River from Lewistown. CHARLES KAY

Building detail, Landusky. MARK MELOY

the veins of gold underground. The Ruby Gulch mine above the town of Zortman became one of the richest mines in Montana, producing more than a million dollars in gold in 1911, as much as $14,000 a day in gold bullion.

The cyanide mill used to process the Ruby Gulch gold burned twice, in 1912 and 1923, but it was rebuilt into one of the few large-scale gold operations to survive in 20th-century Montana. Charles Whitcomb, an early resident of Zortman, organized a group of financiers from Helena and Butte to rebuild the mine in the early 1930s. They constructed what was thought to be the second largest cyanide-leach mill in the world. That operation lasted until the outbreak of World War II, when the mine was forced to

close as the miners were called to the war effort.

The Little Rockies are said to have yielded $25 million in gold before the war. With high precious-metals prices in 1984, the annual gold and silver production of a new mine operating above Zortman surpassed the value of all the precious metals wrenched from the Little Rockies during the entire previous century.

This, the largest "heap leach" gold mine in the world, was opened in 1979 to renew mining in the range. Obliterating the tunnels, shacks and heaps of the previous century, the Zortman-Landusky open-pit mine ripped the lid off the mountain tops to gather 18 million tons of ore, producing 291,000 ounces of gold and 640,000 ounces of silver in its first five years of production.

The process of gold recovery is a tremendous but simple one. Ore yielding only an ounce of gold per 50-ton truckload is hauled from the pit where it had been blasted into rubble. It is piled atop a gargantuan, impermeable pad. A solution of cyanide and water sprinkled over the pile saturates the ore and dissolves its gold and silver minerals. Gravity carries the precious minerals in solution to the bottom, and the "pregnant" cyanide solution is pumped to a mill where the metals are precipitated from it and refined into bullion.

In 1984 the mine began construction of "super pads" capable of receiving ore that fills many acres in the bowl-shaped mountain drainage below the mine. The expanded operation allows the company to adjust its operation to the vagaries of the

gold market. When the price of gold declines, mining can be halted while production continues from the huge reserves. Production costs are thus reduced without interrupting the output of bullion.

A century of mining in the Little Rockies carries a heavy impact on aesthetics and on the continued well-being of other resources. Great avalanches of mine wastes have spilled into the gulches, clogging channels and polluting springs. Despite such disruptions, thousands of people flock to the BLM campgrounds annually to enjoy these prairie mountains. Keep the kids away from the spring gurgling past the picnic tables at Montana Gulch: the sign warns that it is not fit for consumption. The Zortman-Landusky Mine lies at its headwaters

Charles M. Russell's painting "When Loops and Swift Horses Are Surer than Lead" was based on a true incident, which took place farther from the Little Rockies than Russell shows, in the Larb Hills at the head of Larb Creek and Timer Creek. See story on page 50. COURTESY OF AMON CARTER MUSEUM, FT. WORTH

the mountains of central

Christianity was brought to central Montana by a portly, asthmatic Belgian missionary who, in the company of converted Flathead and Nez Perce Indians, made his way into the Judith Basin in 1846. On an altar of buffalo grass, where the Judith joins the Missouri, the priest and his aboriginal attendants offered a mass on the open plains and blessed a throng of 2,000 Blackfeet Indians. Though enemies of the Flathead, the Blackfeet welcomed the litany, as it would expand the scope of their spiritual world and might enhance their power and authority. Believing that the more "medicine" the better, Plains Indians were eclectic in accepting spiritual beliefs.

The priest was Father Pierre-Jean DeSmet, a Jesuit who had organized the first Catholic mission in western Montana's

Father Pierre-Jean DeSmet, 1863-1864. COURTESY MONTANA HISTORICAL SOCIETY

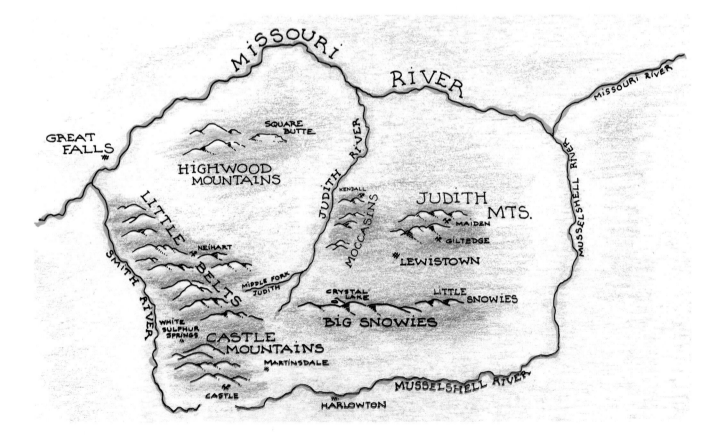

Bitterroot Valley. DeSmet was guided through the Judith Gap between the Little Belt and Snowy mountains along a route known only to the Indians and a few mountain men. In the grand natural cathedral of the low-walled Judith Basin, he bestowed a blessing of peace upon the tribes and unknowingly heralded a flood of immigration that would all but destroy those very people who knelt with him.

Only 20 years later the U.S. Army established Camp Cooke, at the mouth of the Judith, a base from which to send out regular patrols to safeguard the country for settlers. The first trading posts at the mouth of the Musselshell River served steamboat traffic downstream from the burgeoning port at Fort Benton.

In 1873 a trading post known simply as "Post" was established on a creek at the foot of the Big Snowy Mountains, a few miles from what is now Lewistown. In the same year, promoters of the Northern Pacific Railroad laid out the Carroll Trail, a new overland route between the Missouri River and the gold fields. The establishment of trading posts in central Montana accompanied the new route of commerce.

The first permanent settlers were metis, people of French Canadian and Indian blood. Political refugees, they had fled to the States after the first Riel Rebellion, a failed attempt to establish metis land ownership and political sovereignty in Canada. Forty families, their possessions in Red River carts pulled by cattle, arrived to put down the frontier roots of Lewistown. Those "halfbreeds," as they were called, were the distinguished pioneers of Lewistown; the town grew around trade they established.

Fort Maginnis was established at the foot of the Judith Mountains to protect the settlers from Indians who left their reservations and came to the area to hunt as they had for centuries. Even though the wars of the previous decade had left few free-roaming Indians south of the Missouri by this time, the U.S. cavalry maintained high troop levels at Fort Maginnis, a symbol of security to settlers.

Guarding those people and their livestock from the threat of Indian attack—a threat that never was real—were about 250 soldiers at Fort Maginnis. The fort was the last of five built in response to the hysteria that followed the Custer defeat on the Little Bighorn to the southeast. The soldiers who served at Fort Maginnis fought no major battles in the fort's 10-year existence. Ultimately Fort Maginnis became a burden to the federal government and was abandoned in 1890.

The troops were ostensibly to protect open-range cattle spreads like the DHS Ranch, which was locat-

Above: Scouting near Fort Maginnis.
Right: Fort Maginnis at the foot of the Judith Mountains.
PHOTOS COURTESY OF MONTANA HISTORICAL SOCIETY

Above: Granville Stuart, photographed by L.A. Huffman. MONTANA HISTORICAL SOCIETY
Left: An 1885 sketch by Rufus Zogbaum from Harper's New Monthly Magazine, *of Stuart's Stranglers in the Judiths.*

ed near the fort. On the contrary, DHS partner Granville Stuart reported in a letter to another partner, Samuel Hauser of Helena, that the ranch required protection from larcenous soldiers. "Had my hands full or I would have forwarded report ere this," he wrote in a letter quoted in *Not in Precious Metals Alone* (Montana Historical Society, 1976). "On the 3rd a company of soldiers left here for [Fort] Keogh and as two of our men was coming up from below . . . they meets two soldiers who had the hind quarters of a freshly killed beef behind their saddles." The soldiers dodged the ranch hands, who reported the theft to Stuart. The frontier cattle rancher readily admitted that beef rustling by the supposed guardians of the plains was "the regular thing with them and they all do it, and do it

plenty too." Since the ranch was a main supplier of non-rustled beef for the fort, and the DHS relied heavily on government military supply contracts, perhaps Stuart had to tolerate the pilferage.

The handful of open-range cattlemen who settled in Montana in the late 1870s and 1880s found paradise–clean, clear water from the mountains and nutritious native grass on the prairie. They simply released the herds and hired a few cowboys to keep track of the cows, which were as free to roam as had been the buffalo they replaced. The rugged terrain of the Judith Basin sometimes made it difficult to locate range cattle and also aided the escapes of cattle thieves.

Cattle rustling was the black heart of the prairie. The 1884 losses to rustling were five percent in the area

surrounding the Judith Basin. After one debilitating spring raid when rustlers cleaned out the DHS's horse pastures in the Judith Mountains an enraged Granville Stuart took the law into his own hands. With 13 men he rode out after the rustlers and, before the news of the vigilantes even hit the newspapers, the "Stuart's Stranglers" campaign was over. The vigilantes kept quiet about the raids on rustler camps, but later estimates were that between 19 and 75 alleged rustlers had been shot or hanged without benefit of trial.

Author John K. Hutchens in *One Man's Montana*, wrote a somewhat embellished account of one raid. At Bates Point in the Missouri Breaks, the Stranglers laid siege to the cabin hideout of "Stringer Jack's" band of desperados. They attacked at dawn, an intense gun battle ensued and,

"Waiting for a Chinook," by Charles M. Russell, told the story of the "Hard Winter of 1886-1887" with hardly a word.
COURTESY MONTANA STOCKGROWERS ASSOCIATION

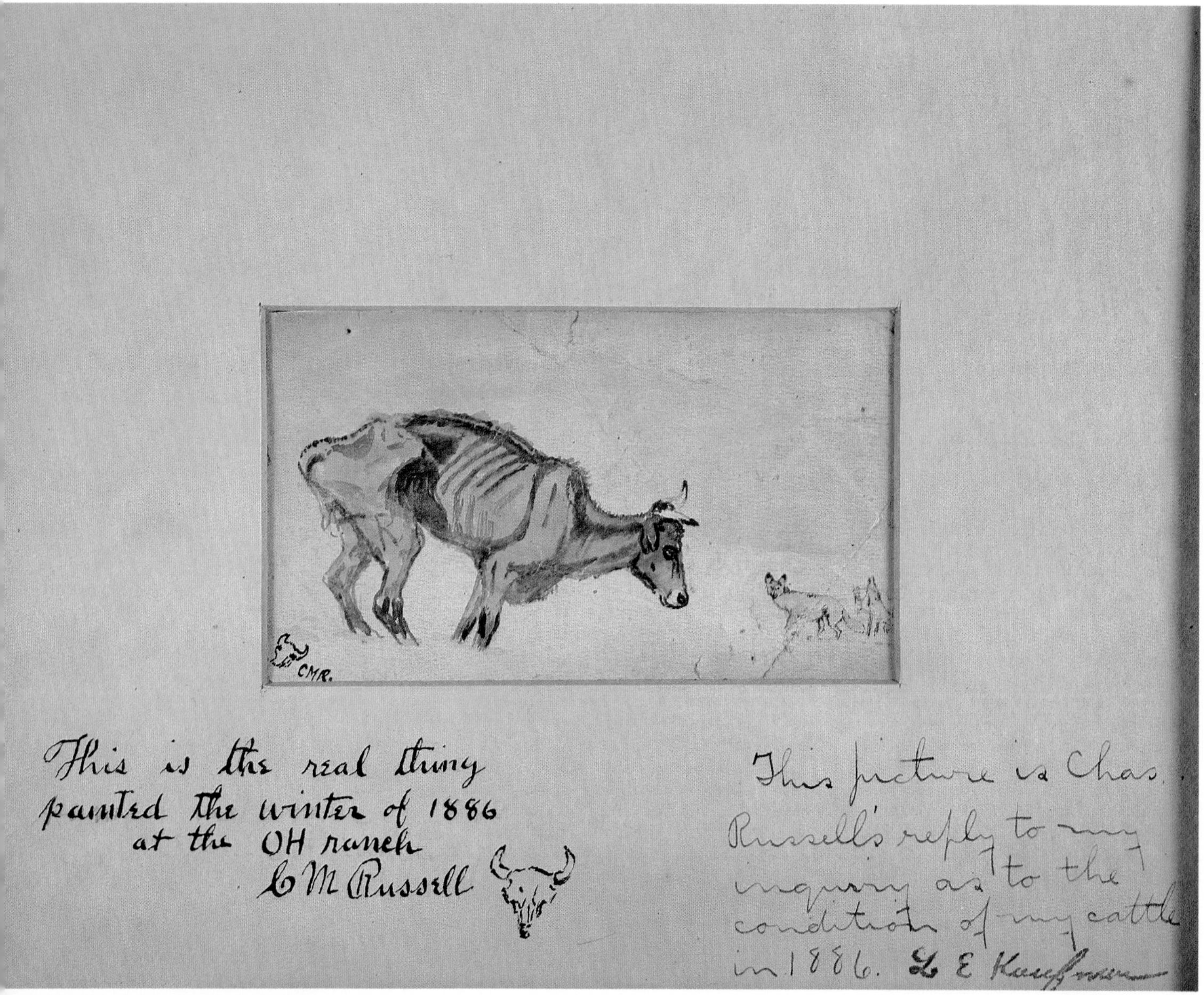

This is the real thing
painted the winter of 1886
at the OH ranch
C M Russell

This picture is Chas.
Russell's reply to my
inquiry as to the
condition of my cattle
in 1886. L E Kaufman

outnumbered, the rustlers were nearly wiped out. Several of the gang shot themselves when the posse set fire to the cabin, preferring suicide to hanging. Three of the rustlers managed to escape downstream on a commandeered raft. One of them was particularly keen to get away, since he was said to be Stuart's nephew.

The vigilantes finally enlisted the aid of the soldiers at Fort Maginnis who, according to Hutchens, wired the Indian police at the Poplar Creek Agency, and the latter picked up the men 200 miles downstream on the Missouri. A U.S. marshal brought the men back to stand trial at Fort Maginnis but was met near the mouth of the Musselshell by a band of hooded riders. The group kidnapped the prisoners and hanged them from a nearby tree.

Because of the distance from central Montana to the nearest authority and because ranchers like Granville Stuart held sway over the state in the 1880s, no formal inquiry was called to discuss the propriety of the vigilantes' efforts. One leading newspaper even went so far as to suggest that Stuart be paid for his efforts. The outlier province was a lawless place, where land barons, sequestered in the protected foothills of the prairie mountains, ruled the surrounding plains like medieval lords.

"Hard Winter" of 1886-1887

Beyond the control of men like Stuart was the weather. Losses to rustling were minute compared to

Maiden, Montana Territory, at the head of Warm Springs Creek in the Judith Mountains. MONTANA HISTORICAL SOCIETY

those suffered in the "Hard Winter" of 1886-1887, when half (estimates vary from 20 percent to 90 percent) the range cattle in the territory died of exposure. The stockmen were not set up to provide hay for the winter feeding of their stock; they relied on the windblown ridges of the outlier country for open grazing through the winter. But a year of low cattle prices and drought had left the prairies overgrazed and in poor shape. A mid-January (1887) thaw, refrozen by the onset of more cold weather, encased the ground with ice and was followed by heavy snows.

"The cattle drifted down on all the rivers, and untold thousands went down the air holes," wrote a cowboy on the DHS, "Teddy Blue" Abbott, in *We Pointed Them North.* On the Missouri we lost I don't know how many that way. They would walk out on the ice, the ones behind would push the front ones in. The cowpunchers worked like slaves to move them back in the hills."

A sketch on the back of a postcard — a gaunt steer hunched over without protection from fierce blowing snow, a coyote at its heels — immortalized that winter. Cowboy Charlie Russell had drawn it in reply to a query about the status of the herd he was working.

The winter ended the era of open-range cattle ranching and revised the notions of its practitioners. "A business that had been fascinating to me before, suddenly became distasteful," wrote Granville Stuart. "I wanted no more of it. I never wanted

to own again an animal that I could not feed and shelter." Nearly 400,000 carcasses lay rotting in the feeble sunlight of spring across Montana.

"Stuart's Stranglers," the cattlemen vigilantes, had ridden out on their missions of self-government from a rough saloon in the Judith Mountains in the spring of 1884. It was in those mountains that the town of Gilt Edge later rose to serve the gold and silver mines that dotted the range in the 1880s. Named for the rim of gold ore found at the edge of a limestone cliff, Gilt Edge boasted a

population of 350 into the 20th century. But by the 1920s, it was completely bust, a ghost town attracting only retired caretakers, grazing cattle and souvenir hunters.

Martha Canary, better known as Calamity Jane, called Gilt Edge her favorite town. When she was there in 1898, it had five saloons, and she claimed to be the town's constable. *The Great Falls Tribune* later published a reminiscence of one of the law-enforcing techniques used in a poker game. As a losing player rose to leave a crooked game, "a deep

voice that spoke from behind me said, 'Stay right where you are young fellow. I'll see that you get a fair play.' It was Calamity Jane and she had a nice little gun pointed right in the middle of the card game." (From Muriel Wolle, *Montana Pay Dirt.)*

Another story is told about the cold winter night when one of the ranchers in the Gilt Edge area gave a big Christmas party, at which the men clearly outnumbered the available dancers—married women and schoolmarms. An ambitious cowboy then invited the local ladies of the

difficult, especially in winter when the accumulation of mountain snows brought activity nearly to a standstill. Attesting to the rigors of life in a mining camp are reports of the deplorable living conditions and violent outlets of social frustration. Most of the men in the mines worked long shifts and were hired and fired at the whims of mine owners. In some cases the workers shared their bunks and as one man came off a shift, the other rolled out of bed and surrendered it to his exhausted cohort.

Finances were precarious for the mountain dwellers. Mismanagement, depleted ore leads and declining prices of the precious metals often meant unmet mine payrolls. Gambling and drinking were rampant during the booms, while an entire town might find its population destitute a month later.

night to give things a little balance. When the women arrived, the rancher ignored his wife's objections and declared, "Well, I don't suppose Jesus would have kicked them out on a night like this." The saloon ladies stayed, and the party was worth remembering.

Although Gilt Edge had a big reputation, the real population center of the Judith Mountains was a town called Maiden. The original prospectors wanted to name the place Groven after an Indian woman, but their minds were changed by a white woman who asked them to name the town for her young daughter, Maiden.

In 1881, 6,000 miners lived in Maiden. Over its 40-year lifespan, more than $5 million in gold was taken from surrounding mines. Maiden's one main street was at the

headwaters of Warm Springs Creek in the Judiths. The narrow confines of that gulch were lined with canvas tents and a host of substantial buildings—an assemblage far larger than the small creek bottom could reasonably accommodate. Maiden had its own newspaper, the *Mineral Argus,* and enough residents to put it in an election competition with Lewistown for county seat in 1882. Capturing the seat of government might have sealed a properous future for Maiden, but the rough little town in a narrow gulch of the Judith Mountains lost to the more central valley location offered by Lewistown.

The permanency to which the prairie-mountain mining towns aspired seldom occurred. Most often, they were temporary camps that faded along with the ore bodies upon which they depended. Life was

Above: Dependence on silver production doomed towns like Kendall in the North Moccasins when government silver policy changed. Left: Drill rock from miners' competitions.
MARK MELOY PHOTOS

Often the men would take out their frustrations on the minority members of the camp. In one situation, reported the *Mineral Argus*, the prey were Maiden's Chinese. Even after several attempts at intimidation, including the posting of a skull and crossbones, the Chinese paid little heed to "hints" that they leave. A party of 30 masked men upped the stakes.

"Gee R. Joe," the January 14, 1886, *Argus* reported, "Montana Street laundryman, was first visited and apprised of the fact that the hour of his departure had arrived and any unnecessary delay would not be conducive to longevity. Joe started for Lewistown accompanied by four other Chinamen who had been admonished by the klan to go hence."

Its moral fiber and mines played out, Maiden fell into complete physical disrepair, and most of its buildings were gutted by fire in 1906.

Kendall, Neihart and Castle

By 1900, the mines had been moved across the valley into the North Moccasin Mountains. Harry Kendall, an innovative miner who had put together some capital by reworking abandoned mines in the Judiths, built a mine and mill that would yield $2.5 million in its first five years. Where others of his time had failed, he succeeded by recovering microscopic amounts of gold from crushed ore dissolved in a cyanide solution. The pure gold was then milled by a relatively simple procedure.

The growth of the town of Kendall was phenomenal. The mine made Fergus County the state's leading gold producer by 1914, and the town sported a new stone-block hotel that had 26 rooms, hot water, hot-air

City of Neihart, 1891, Little Belt Mountains, survived until well after the turn of the century.
MONTANA HISTORICAL SOCIETY

heating and electricity. In 1906 the Kendall Mine was sold to a group from Butte and New York City, who doubled the investment through offerings on the stock market.

The new owners upgraded the property and hired 200 more miners. An opera house was built beside two banks and numerous saloons and mercantile establishments. Under company guidance the community vied with Lewistown as the new center of commerce in Fergus County.

Kendall miners listened to some radical political ideas when the local miners' union held its annual spring celebration in 1902. One speaker at the banquet offered the notion that "the United States would be best served by the government owning the railroads and other pub-

lic utilities, and that a socialistic system should supplant the present order of things." (Quoted by Muriel Wolle in *Montana Pay Dirt.*) Often thought of as the backwaters of industrial society, western mining towns like Kendall tried to be on the cutting edge of national politics.

By 1925 the workers of glorious Kendall abandoned that drainage high in the Moccasins. The ornate Victorian bandstand in that remote corner of the frontier, from which orators had admonished the world to change, became a granary for a farm in the valley below.

Even compared to the boom-and-bust cycle characteristic of mining towns, the 1890s were especially severe for towns based on silver production as that metal's value plum-

meted. Neihart, however, was the anomaly. Deep in the Little Belts, remote from other towns, it benefited from a late start in the silver mining business. Although an active mining population had been there in 1881, travel into the steep narrow canyon had been limited to a rough trail. Ten years later, a railway line from Great Falls was completed. The train was greeted by the usual hoopla: the Neihart Free Coinage Brass Band performed and everyone got drunk. Providing the legend that would mark the day in the annals of frontier history, "Jew Jake" got his leg shot off by a law officer named Treat.

With the arrival of the railway Neihart had the means to industrialize, and other mining towns in the Little Belts abandoned their populations to its greener pastures. When, among other things, Congress voted to cease the government's monopoly on the silver market in 1893, Neihart's boom busted—but only briefly. Still rich in silver ore and production machinery, the town was saved by William A. Clark, one of Butte's infamous copper kings. Clark bought up the mines and had the financial means to keep them in production.

Though it experienced periods of depression, Niehart was always ready to resume production when the price of silver rose. It maintained an ephemeral existence; when silver prices went up, the ghosts were shooed out and the miners returned. Though railroad service ceased 40 years ago, Neihart

is yet poised to resume production.

Before the silver crash of 1893, Castle had nine stores, a bank, two barber shops and butcher shops, livery barns, hotels, a photo gallery, dancehall, church, schoolhouse, jail, 14 saloons and seven brothels. During its 10-year lifespan, it had four different newspapers. Its streets were jammed with activity. Four daily stagecoaches competed for passage on the narrow mountain roads with freighters and bull teams hauling ore, fuel and mining machinery.

When it became clear that Castle needed a railroad, entrepreneur Richard Harlow stepped forward to build the Montana Railroad from the huge smelter in East Helena to the state's richest silver mines at Castle. The Cumberland Mine had

6,000 tons of silver ore waiting for delivery, and smelter owners were offering a bonus of $250,000 as Harlow's incentive to build the Jawbone.

Called the "Jawbone" because of Harlow's ability to be "long on talk and short on funds," the railroad posed an enormous challenge. With only $25,000 to start construction in 1893, Harlow used unemployed Helena miners to build the railroad up the Missouri River to Sixteen Mile Creek near Toston. He provided his workers only the necessities of food, shelter and clothing, issuing IOUs for wages payable when the line reached Castle several years later.

His money spent and the price of silver falling, Harlow had a difficult time raising the funds to complete the line. Castle, in the meantime,

was well on its way to becoming a ghost town. Against all financial odds, Harlow begged and borrowed his way up the steep canyon of Sixteen Mile Creek:

"We had a frightful time getting supplies up Sixteen Mile Creek," Harlow told the Richland County *Leader* in 1922. "A four-horse team with oats was sent to a camp from Toston and landed without a pound of oats in the wagon. It was caught in a snowstorm and the driver had to feed all the oats to the horses. The owners of little ranches we crossed held us up with shotguns. Ranchmen hesitated to sell us supplies, fearing they wouldn't get their money."

Given Harlow's reputation, the ranchers' suspicions were well founded. Yet somehow he had built

Construction of the Montana Railroad, better known as the "Jawbone" for its developer's reputation of being "long on talk and short on funds," connected East Helena and Castle. MONTANA HISTORICAL SOCIETY

his railroad into Castle by 1897. By then, there was little else to haul but the stocks of silver ore that had been stored over the life of the mines in anticipation of the completion of the rail line. Mining had ceased, and the price of silver was at a disastrous low.

Harlow received little for his efforts, and his debts were high. Nevertheless he continued his career as a railroad magnate. From Lennep he built eastward and linked into the rail lines of the Northern Pacific Railroad at Lewistown by 1903. In a last bid to make his fortune, he suggested a sale of the Jawbone to the Northern Pacific. His sales pitch included made-up names of towns served by the line, such as "Fanalulu" below Ringling, a

contrived combination of two lady friends' names. He even had the names printed on train schedules.

The Northern Pacific did not buy, but the Jawbone was sold a few years later to the Chicago, Milwaukee, St. Paul and Pacific Railroad. Harlow claimed that his debts were settled with the proceeds of the sale, leaving little profit. One of the first things the new owners did was to tear out the spur line serving the ghost town of Castle.

Transportation was always the key to frontier resource development. The building of railroads into the prairie mountains was a marginal investment, but the lines connecting them across the broad valleys of central Montana would eventually pay off. The settlers who

followed the miners would foot the bill for earlier transportation failures.

The turn-of-the-century mining camps in the Little Belts, Castles and Judiths were only the initial stage of settlement. Later immigrants relied on the web of transportation established by mining and took up the land along these routes. Often the hordes did not stay long, but they always kept coming for the riches of the new frontier.

Except for seasonal forays for building materials and wild game, those who came to homestead and to found the permanent agricultural base of central Montana largely ignored the prairie mountains. For them, the outliers existed largely for their extractable resources: one went there to get something, and that something usually was not consumed in the mountains, but was hauled elsewhere for use. Early in this century, forest fires burned unchecked in the outliers, huge torches seen for hundreds of miles across the prairie. Scarred by mining and charred by wildfire, the mountains held no interest for settlers. The outliers of central Montana reverted to the custody of the federal government, particularly the Forest Service and the Bureau of Land Management, in whose care they would remain. Eventually the forests would recover, the all-important watersheds would endure.

The Castle Mountains' town of Castle in 1888.
MONTANA HISTORICAL SOCIETY

the mountains of central

The ghost town of Castle. RICK GRAETZ

Castle Mountains

Fanning out from all sides of the Castle Mountains, Willow, Four Mile, Bonanza, Alabaugh and Warm Springs creeks water the Smith and Musselshell rivers, tributaries that enter the Missouri River 200 miles apart. The watershed is a cluster of small peaks rising from the river valleys between the Crazy and Little Belt mountains.

Towering outcrops of granite and limestone on the range's west end are laid bare by millennia of abrasion from wind, rain and snow. Set off by the surrounding velvet-green forest canopy, these white pinnacles seem, from a distance, to be nearly translucent when the slanted evening light strikes them.

The most prominent building in White Sulphur Springs, the town at the base of the Castles, is said to be an architectural mirror of the natural "castles" of the mountains. Old Stone Castle, now the three-story

Castle
Judith
Moccasin

Snowy
Highwood
Little Belt Mountains

Square and Round Buttes

Stone formations like these seen at a distance suggest the Castle Mountains' name.

The Castles at Horse Park. MARK MELOY PHOTOS

Meagher County Museum, was built by B.R. Sherman, an early entrepreneur who derived much of his fortune from mining in the mountains.

Precious metals from the Castles attracted some of the first immigrants to the upper Musselshell Valley in the 1880s, and remnants of those days are scattered across the landscape. It is difficult to walk or drive anywhere in the east end of the range without coming upon some relic of mining— prospect holes overgrown by spindly lodgepole pine,

heavy pieces of rusted metal discarded when mines played out and mills closed.

The Castles' slopes once sprouted mining camps teeming with people. The most prominent, appropriately dubbed Castle Town, has fallen to ruin, but many of its more substantial buildings remain, listing under the weight of a century. A hand-hewn beam, an ornate arrangement of shingles and filigree along the eaves, show the signs of skilled craft. What is left of the drooping, weathered buildings, not carted off

during decades of vandalism, is propped up on the hillside, the tombstones of an era.

Almost nothing is left of Robinson and Copperopolis high in the Castles. The valley towns of Martinsdale, Two Dot, Harlowton and White Sulphur Springs prospered as agriculture claimed the upper Musselshell.

A few families survived the transition by adjusting to a quixotic economy. Kay Berg's grandfather came to Castle at the turn of the century and ran the butcher shop. When the

mines played out, he and his family moved down the valley to the small railroad town of Lennep. They eventually settled in Martinsdale and opened a store.

Today, Kay Berg operates a garage in Martinsdale and makes his home in the building that was the family store until ranchers started going into White Sulphur Springs for groceries. The small-town grocery declined as ranching became less labor-intensive, Berg believes, and as sheep ranching in the valleys surrounding the Castles declined. He

Bull elk testing his tines. ED WOLFF

remembers when 20 bands of a thousand sheep each grazed in the Castles; the sheep herders alone were enough to keep the store alive.

Berg once ran a mine in the Castles to supplement his income. Whenever the price of silver and lead justified it, he worked the Lucky Dollar Mine. With the prices of those metals only a fraction of what they were 10 years ago, the work is hardly profitable. Berg's "hired help" — his sons — have grown and left home, and Berg now intends to sell the mine.

He may sell the property but cannot as easily market the know-how it takes to operate the small mine. "It's a dying art," he said. "When guys like us are gone, people will have forgotten how to operate a small mine."

The small miners of recent times, an "endangered species," have covered the east end of the Castles with roads. But in the unroaded west end of the range, a wildlife biologist could not design better habitat for elk. "It's an elk paradise," according to George Cameron, timber specialist for the U.S. Forest Service.

The west end of the Castles is likely to remain a sanctum for elk and wildness because it is rugged. A system of primitive trails passes through meadows, surrounded by a dark forest of nearly impenetrable stands of lodgepole pine and Douglas fir. The mix of meadow and forest — and their roadlessness – make ideal elk habitat.

It is a place where humans might encounter an elk if they are willing to hike into the twilight of a long summer evening along a tunnel-like path through the timber. Suddenly, you leave the darkened corridor of trees and enter a bright meadow like a mysterious room where someone just turned on the lights. The park is resplendent with wildflowers and knee-high grasses. Grazing cattle have not made their way into this high country, and it remains pristine. You drink from bubbling springs without fear.

Waiting on the edge of the next meadow in the darkness of the trees, a young bull appears, every step cautious and deliberate. He senses you but will not flee until he is certain. His shape, the hump at his shoulders and the swaying neck, bring to mind a camel crossing the desert. Inadvertently or through curiosity, his slow steps are in your direction, close enough to see the glistening brown velvet on his growing spikes.

Suddenly he stomps a hoof, bellows his unearthly call and weaves, unwilling to relinquish the meadow. You move into the open, and the elk marches away stiff-legged, hooves drumming the sod of the meadow. He turns and bellows once again the shrill drone that reverberates against the mountain walls. It is an encounter you do not readily forget.

Though undeniably wild, the Castles probably will not become part of the nation's system of congressionally protected wilderness in the near future. The Forest Service plans to leave the country alone for the present decade. Of course, those plans can change. The future of wildness in the Castle Mountains is uncertain.

Mining technologies and the price of silver to a large extent will dictate the Castles' future. If the miners see fit to reactivate the hundreds of claims in the Castles, there is little to stop them short of repealing mining laws more than a century old.

For the present, the west end of the Castles will see disruption only by cattle, an occasional motorcycle, a rancher on horseback, a cross-country skier or the errant photographer.

Judith and Moccasin Mountains

The corpulent ridges and fertile fields of central Montana curve around Lewistown and open into a vast bowl known as the Judith Basin. The Northern Plains and the portals of the Rockies merge into a gentle land where the rich glacial soils of the prairie are watered by precipitation and runoff nurtured by the low mountains.

North of town, in a cluster shaped like a crescent moon, the Judith Mountains give birth to the springs that irrigate valley hay crops when summer rains disappear. The streams radiate from the Judiths and neighboring Moccasin Mountains like spokes on a wheel whose rim is a line following the Judith, Musselshell and Missouri rivers.

Percolating from the igneous core of the Judiths, in the forested bowl between 6,400-foot Judith Peak and 6,000-foot Pekay Peak, Warm Springs Creek gathers a foamy head but promptly disappears in limestone sinks as it exits the mountains. Its scantily watered channel proceeds west to breach the gap that separates the Moccasin Mountains into its north and south flanks. From here, replenished by a large spring, the rejuvenated stream continues a circuitous route toward the sluggish meanders of the Judith River. Laying bare the rich loam of the basin along its banks, the Judith drains northward into the Missouri.

At the mouth of the Judith, on May 29, 1805, Captain William Clark of the Lewis and Clark Expedition admired the "handsome" stream and, by extension, the mountains, naming them after his 13-year-old cousin in Virginia, whom he would marry four years later.

The Judith Mountains received its first major white settlements only in the 1880s. Leading the way was the DHS Ranch of A.J. Davis, Samuel Hauser and Granville Stuart, headquartered on Ford's Creek at the southeast flank of the range. The subsequent mining boom spawned towns like Maiden, and expansive construction at Fort Maginnis, a few miles upstream from the DHS Ranch, signaled a burgeoning regional population. As the initial boom of settlement thinned out, about 2,000 people were residents of the Judith Mountains, in the hamlets of Andersonville, Alpine and New Year. By 1883 there were 33,000 head of cattle within a 20-mile radius of Maiden.

Lewistown, home today to about 10,000 people, followed Maiden as the prominent town of the Judith Basin. Longtime newspaper publisher Ken Byerly is proud that his Lewistown *News-Argus* traces its lineage back to the Maiden *Mineral Argus* of a hundred years ago. The semi-weekly *Argus* maintains a keen interest in keeping its historic roots alive, recording the family histories of hundreds of basin residents through the years.

Curious to see just how great was his readers' interest in local history, Byerly once wrote in a column that he would send anyone who asked a square nail from the ruins of Fort Maginnis. To his great astonishment, the requests flooded in.

More recently, Byerly wrote a story that grew to legendary proportions. In the summer of 1971, Puppy, a "sad eyed" mongrel "with a bit of collie in it" was abandoned by the side of the road below Maiden. Rancher Bill Koza saw the dog sitting by the road near his house and ran him off several times. But the dog always returned to the same spot. Koza could see the dog was starving; the animal even tried to catch mice to eat.

For a full year and through a hard winter, the dog maintained his vigil beside the road waiting for his master to return. Koza built a shelter for "Puppy," and he and others regularly put out food. No one could approach and pet the dog.

"Abandoned Dog Keeps Lonely Vigil," ran the *News-Argus* headline. The story and accompanying photo-

graph were so heart-rending, they could have made a mass murderer weep. The Associated Press wire service picked up the story, and Puppy's plight appeared in scores of newspapers across the country. Letters rolled in from all over the United States and Canada. According to Byerly, "People sent money, poems and even a Valentine for Puppy."

Puppy eventually became Bill Koza's pet, but he died when hit by a car not long afterward. Even after more than 10 years, Koza still receives letters, so devoted were Puppy's many fans.

In addition to his duties as the scribe of central Montana, Byerly is an ardent booster of community projects. He and several other Lewistown citizens are members of a committee formed several years ago to improve the recreational potential of the Judith Mountains.

The fertile grassland on the east end of the Judiths offered irresistible pasturage to frontier ranchers like Granville Stuart. MARK MELOY PHOTOS

Above: Armells Creek from the top of Red Mountain in the Judiths.
Right: A reconstructed bandstand at Kendall in the Moccasin Mountains.
MARK MELOY PHOTOS

grounds atop the peaks.

Though little remains of them, the ghost towns lure frequent visitors to the mountains. The town of Kendall once boasted substantial, two-story stone buildings. Today only a few listing walls and naked foundations remain. A wonderfully reconstructed bandstand beside a huge boulder honeycombed with drill holes tells the story that Kendall once sported lively holidays of music and contests of mining prowess.

The best-preserved surviving historic site in the area is one of the oldest, having been built in 1880. When Granville Stuart left the ranching business after the "Hard Winter of 1886-87," he went on to become the foreman of the huge Maginnis Mine in the Judiths. The DHS Ranch was eventually sold, and the original buildings were abandoned. The headquarters of what was one of the largest open-range cattle operations in Montana's hisory are now dilapidated but protected from vandalism because they lie amidst the hay fields of a private ranch. They remain to tell a fading story of life on the frontier.

Snowy Mountains

The Snowy Mountains rise on the prairie between Roundup and Lewistown like a whale gently rolling its shapely back in the midst of a grassland sea. The 100,000-acre bulge of upthrust limestone does not feature the steep, craggy, cloud-raking peaks of the Rockies. Instead the Snowies are capped with an eight-mile-long meadow, a nearly flat surface that goes on and on, east to west, as if designed especially for the walker who seeks views rather than long, grunting ascents. From atop the Snowies, on the whale's smooth back, those views stretch into Canada to the north and

south all the way into the Yellowstone country, an expanse of 300 miles.

The Snowies' north flank benefits from storms that bear enough precipitation to support dense stands of lodgepole pine and Douglas fir. In contrast, the south side lies in a rain shadow. This dry, rocky, exposed ridgeline rises three thousand feet above the dry prairie. Its huge, bowl-shaped drainages cut the craggy southern face of the Snowies like the edge of a serrated knife, forming what is appropriately called Knife Blade Ridge.

Though water is scarce, several small streams emerge from the

south side of the Snowies – Blake and Timber creeks, Swimming Woman and Careless creeks. At the head of Blake Creek a narrow shaft in a limestone outcrop leads to Big Ice Cave, whose cool sculptures of accumulated ice provide an air-conditioned room that is the destination of many hikers during the

Wading through red tape for years, the group succeeded in obtaining a government appropriation to dismantle obsolete Air Force radar installations atop Judith Peak and Red Mountain. During the summer of 1985, the Bureau of Land Management was directing the construction and maintenance of new picnic

summer. When the outside temperature is 90 degrees, temperatures down in Big Ice Cave can be 40 degrees cooler.

The Snowies' eastern end narrows and here Knife Blade Ridge lives up to its name. Following a trail-wide precipice that falls steeply on either side, the ridge skirts the high points of the range — Greathouse Peak (8,681 feet) and Old Baldy (8,678

south of Lewistown. A clean camping space can be claimed for a small fee that helps maintain a resident Forest Service employee during the summer, when visitation is at its peak. Most visitors use the campground as a base for short day-hikes to the ridgetop. More adventuresome hikers will carry sufficient water for an overnight camp atop the ridge.

In recent years the Snowies have

without signing the trail register at Big Ice Cave atop the ridge.

The Snowy Mountains are not only a place of recreation. Their foothills, reached by roads that vary from gravelled to graded to someone's faint memory, are places for living and working.

One October day a few years ago, I chose a gravel road off Highway 87 between Roundup and Grassrange

grasslands edge against the mountains.

Driving along the terraces of lower Willow Creek, I passed only a few houses, most of which looked as if they had been abandoned for decades. Well grazed stretches of gray-brown rangeland lay in stark contrast to strips of newly plowed land gleaming with vibrant green shoots of winter wheat. Closer to the mountains, Willow Creek emerged from the canyons that carved the low ridgeline. This sluggish brown flow of alkaline water, which an unknowing walker might step over without much notice, was the lifeblood of the country.

On this remote prairie, the fallow grain fields fatten lambs into someone's Christmas roast. Bands of more than a thousand sheep move through the fields like four-legged vacuum cleaners, voraciously gobbling stray heads of grain missed by the huge harvesting machines that passed through earlier in the season.

When the sheep moved down to the creek at mid-day for a drink and a rest, I had the opportunity to visit with herder Joe Brooks. A stocky, bearded man in his forties, wrapped in several layers of worn wool garments, Brooks has the look of one whose life is hard and vigorous, but satisfying. He is responsible for his employer's huge investment of livestock. He tends to their health, moves them to good grass and protects them from coyotes. Herding has been his livelihood for the last 12 years.

Life as a herder is an extraordinarily spartan affair, requiring a strong constitution and an affinity for solitude. For Joe, it also means living in a century-old, primitive sheep-wagon home where a person

Looking over Beaver Creek Valley toward the South Moccasin Mountains. TOM DIETRICH

feet). Beyond, it drops into a series of canyons and ultimately into a saddle where the lower ridges–the Little Snowies–veer northeast for 15 miles.

Most visitors take on the Big Snowies from the north side, beginning at the Forest Service campground at Crystal Lake, 25 miles

been the destination of hordes of weekenders from Billings and Great Falls, often overflowing the campgrounds at Crystal Lake. Locals and veteran Snowy Mountain hikers know they need only amble up the steep trail to the ridge to escape the hubbub. Many a Lewistown family will not let the summer go by

and aimed my truck in the general direction of a narrow notch in the south face of the Little Snowies. If I could decipher the map's hieroglyphics of jumbled county roads and could make the right choices at frequent intersections, I hoped ultimately to find a sheepherder friend who lived year-round where the

can barely lean over to tie his shoe.

An unannounced but welcomed guest, I escaped the incessant autumn wind and slid in next to Joe on the bench inside the wagon. With his knee practically against it, he stoked the tiny woodstove and moved the blackened coffee pot to more direct heat.

Opposite the bench were the accouterments of a kitchen. Far too many blackened pots lined the shelves next to the woodstove, which coated everything in the wagon with soot.

As the wind gently rocked the heavy wagon, and a thin shaft of afternoon sunlight slanted in from the open top of the Dutch door, Joe pulled down some of his possessions from the shelf and bunk above us. One was a black felt hat purchased on his last trip to town a few months back. Although it was a bit large and bent his ears over when he pulled it on, the hat was the object of great pride. Next came the heavy,

holstered six-shooter, a .44 magnum whose bullets looked big enough to pulverize a bowling ball at ten paces. He handed the gun to me as one might cradle an infant.

As we finished our coffee, Joe detailed his dream of constructing a new wagon atop a two-ton truck. This home would give him more room to move around, he said and, no doubt, better places to store his treasures–the hat and gun, a clock,

a kerosene lamp, a dog-eared collection of Wild West books and magazines and, perhaps most important, his radio. From it came the sounds of a country-music station in Billings, a constant diet of Mickey Gilley, Conway Twitty, Willie and Dolly.

When we buy our lamb chops, most of us have no idea that people like Joe Brooks work to produce them–people who live most of their

Top left: Old Baldy in the Big Snowies. TOM DIETRICH *Bottom left:* A thousand sheep move to bedground on the Snowy Mountain Ranch. MARK MELOY PHOTOS. *Above:* Wild turkeys have been released in several eastern Montana mountain ranges, including the Snowies. ROBERT BREWER

lives outside in the harsh light, chill, heat and ceaseless wind that would drive out the faint-hearted in short order. It is a wilderness with no official recognition beyond the lives touched by it.

Equally as comfortable in a hobo camp or a cattleman's meeting, Joe is distinctly dissimilar to the myth of the Western "Marlboro man." In fact, few times in my travels to the ranch lands of central and eastern Montana have I found that type. Instead, the leather vests over neatly-pressed gingham shirts and the hats elaborately adorned with dyed chicken feathers from Japan are worn by newcomers or "dudes" on their way to weekend rodeos. From land baron to hired help, the tasks

of ranching know few stereotypes beyond hard work, coveralls, floppy hats, and thread-bare clothing invariably stained by a mosaic of a life immersed in blood, oil and manure.

The contrast among users of the Snowy Mountains is remarkable. The wealthy urbanite at Crystal Lake in his $40,000 mobile home escapes to the lush forest for a few days of relaxation. Just over the ridge are people like Joe Brooks, barely surviving but not aware of any particular need to escape.

Top: Wildlflowers carpet the crest of the Snowies in late June.
MARK MELOY

Bottom: The Snowies' Crystal Lake is a magnet to the folks in Lewistown.
TOM DIETRICH

Highwood Mountains

Rising above swaying shafts of wheat, the blue knobs of the Highwood Mountains ripple in the heat waves of a summer afternoon. Few people explore those abrupt domes south of the smooth terraces below the Missouri River; for most, the Highwoods are a soothing part of the landscape around Great Falls, Fort Benton and Belt.

Strips of gold and black, grain and fallow, alternate along the roadsides that cut the broad plain of the Golden Triangle, its soils furrowed into the most productive wheat fields anywhere. The country is immense, dominated by the curvature of the earth and the sky that meets it.

The Highwoods interrupt that immense plain at the northern extremity of a chain of island ranges. With the Crazies, Castles and Little Belts, they parallel the mainstem Rockies like a reef following the ocean shoreline. Geologists hypothesize that, as the northern abutment of that line of igneous ridges, the Highwoods actually halted the southern advance of continental glaciers 30,000 years ago. The thick plate of ice covered much of Canada and for a time actually diverted the flow of the Missouri River to the foot of the Highwoods. A dry falls in the old river channel on the prairie below the range is clearly visible from the top of Square Butte, a prominent Highwoods landmark.

Blackfeet Indians spotted buffalo from lookouts in the Highwoods and sought spiritual guidance there, sitting atop lonely spires, fasting, awaiting dreams and visions. Lewis and Clark, on their expedition in 1805, used the range to mark their progress up the Missouri River, charting their location on a horizon otherwise devoid of obvious landmarks. Homesteaders settled the broad plain but were drawn to the mountains for timber and fuel.

Today, east out of Great Falls, 10th Avenue South flows in the direction of the Highwoods like a glacier of commerce bound for Lewistown, a hundred miles away. After three miles, a paved county road veers toward the Highwoods. Eventually turning to gravel, it climbs up Highwood Creek, fording it a half dozen times, passes over the range and winds down another major drainage, Arrow Creek.

About the Square Buttes:

The large feature south of Great Falls (left) and the butte covered in this book as part of the Highwood Mountains (above) are called Square Butte. The two often are confused because both are locally referred to as "Charlie Russell's Square Butte." In fact, Russell used both of them in backgrounds of his art, but neither is officially known by his name.

Square Butte in Cascade County from Ulm Pishkun. KRISTI DuBOIS

In all, that road bisects 70 square miles of Forest Service land surrounding a half dozen small inholdings of private property. Roughly eight by 13 miles, the area is a mosaic of timber, rocky slopes and meadows–mostly meadows. Twelve peaks hover in a tight group, all near 7,000 feet. Highwood Baldy tops the rest at 7,600 feet.

At the turn of the century the Highwood forest burned. Today the evidence of that fire has disappeared under firm stands of nearly mature lodgepole pine, Douglas fir and limber pine. To the chagrin of range and livestock managers, the regrowth from that fire expands the total forest at a rate of one percent a year, gobbling up meadow grazing lands. To compensate for the loss and protect the grazing resources, the Forest Service prescribes "controlled burns" on a thousand acres of Highwood timber each year. More than 1,600 cattle are fattened each summer on these government grasses.

Hunters also seek a chance at one of the range's beasts. As small as the range may seem, it supports more than 800 elk, and the competition to shoot them is intense. In a recent season, 9,000 applicants sought 300 permits. Sixty percent of those who get the coveted permits come home with meat enough to fill a freezer.

During the summer, 300 youths gather at Camp Arrow Peak, just down the road from the heavily used Forest Service Campground at Thane Creek. Here, the Montana Farmer's Union, an important agricultural organization in the state since 1916, operates its 151-acre camp for young people. Though the kids have a lot of fun, the camp experience is grounded in education. "It's a chance to get the kids off the farm, to get to know each other and to learn some new things about farm management and cooperative marketing," said camp director Judy Doheny.

Rain can provoke gloom in the most stalwart young camper, but these kids have a different attitude about weather. "You have to remember these are farm kids, who think to themselves, 'Hooray for the rain, now Dad can plant his winter wheat this fall,' " Doheny said.

The young people also learn about the mountains in which their camp is located. They might travel over to the Bureau of Land Management's Square Butte Natural Area, isolated miles east of the Highwoods' main cluster. The butte is connected to the Highwoods by ridges capped with long spines of igneous rock, a wall-like formation of blocks that look as if they had been laid by masons. Molten rock injected into the sediments of the earth's crust 50 million years ago cracked the bedrock in much the same way as a board splits when too big a nail is driven into it. The molten rock then filled those cracks and hardened. It now lies exposed as rock walls radiating from the main intrusion, Square Butte.

The Bureau of Land Management protects 2,000 acres of Square Butte, preserving natural attributes such as the relict species of prairie grasses on the butte's flat top. In small patches, interspersed with the thick cover of low timber, are stands of native grass that never have been grazed by domestic livestock. They remain as remnants of the virgin grasses that once covered the vast plains from the Dakotas to the Rockies.

Cowboy artist Charlie Russell placed Square Butte in the backgrounds of many of his paintings, heightening the dramas of his action scenes. (He also painted the other Square Butte, south of Great Falls.) In reality, the majesty of the mile-high, angular plateau is made more compelling by the expanse of prairie flowing from its foot.

Climbing the precipitous sides of the butte is an arduous but not difficult task for a healthy walker, who will be treated to the sight of a bizarre collection of rock formations. The coarse, dark faces of the radiating igneous cliffs seem more akin to canyon features than to mountain topography. Springs trickle and race over slabs of bedrock slanting toward contorted pillars and mushroom-shaped columns resembling the brickwork ruins of an ancient civilization.

Square Butte attracts a variety of wildlife. Occasionally elk from the Highwoods will wander over in search of new territory. Numerous species of birds find homes in the rocky cliffs, including the rare prairie falcon, golden eagles and great horned owls. Of special interest to the managers of the wild area are 25 mountain goats, the progeny of several animals moved to the butte in the early 1970s.

It seems natural that such a distinct landmark would evoke great possessiveness by those in whose landscape and psyche it so prominently figures. Residents of Geraldine and Square Butte, small farm towns nearby, enjoy a running feud over claims to the view. "If I couldn't wake up in the morning and see Square Butte," said Geraldine resident Bill Reeves in the Lewistown *News-Argus*, "I wouldn't think I was home." Folks in his town are luckier than those in Square Butte because, "They live right under it and can't see it so well."

Square Butte appreciates Geraldine's appreciation, but disagrees. Bill Reeves' nephew, John Peters, who was born in Square Butte, says that his uncle should concede that Square Butte's view is better than Geraldine's. "As a matter of fact, Bill comes over here every once in a while to get a better look and to have a drink of our water that is so much tastier than that stuff they have to drink in Geraldine."

Little Belts

"These mountains are just too big to be tamed," said the logger I met on Dead Horse Creek in the Little Belts. His words called to mind a 19th-century frontier attitude, still embraced by some in modern times: The appearance of infinite resources is reason to sanction large-scale resource extraction. Like a sprawling mineral garden and woodlot to some of Montana's major urban centers, the million-acre prairie range indeed seems an endless treasure chest. The Little Belts should enter into any discussion of the largest and most important Montana mountain ranges. Southeast of Great Falls, they sprawl over forested land

Round Butte from Square Butte, Highwood Mountains. JIM ROMO

extending 70 air miles west to east, from the Smith River to Judith Gap, and 60 miles north-south across the two main roads that split them. Broad, not tall and ragged like the peaks of the main Rockies, only a handful of the ridges in the Little Belts are above 8,000 feet.

The Little Belts' long, low forests, lavish meadows, sweeping ridges and a few tiny mountain lakes comprise a critical watershed for central Montana. No less than four major Missouri River tributaries are fed by creeks running from the range's flanks: Belt Creek on the north end, numerous creeks entering the Smith River to the west and the feeders and springs that reach the Musselshell and Judith rivers to the south and east.

The densely forested, shallow, sloping drainages have long been

coveted by lumbermen. Primitive roads wriggle about the range like a can of worms spilled across the map. Parts of the forest that were clearcut and replanted 30 years ago contain new trees six to eight inches in diameter. This is fairly successful reforestation, compared to forests on the arid east side of the Rockies, where trees often take more than a hundred years to mature. The range's sheer size absorbs some of the heavy roading, interspersing it with pockets of wild. The eternal question, of course, is how the wild values survive against the perpetual grind of development. Administrators of the Lewis and Clark National

The Lick Creek area of the Little Belts Mountains. JOHN REDDY

Belt Creek, Little Belt Mountains. JOHN REDDY

Geraldine community get-together in the shadow of the Highwood Mountains. MARK MELOY

Forest believe the resources of the Little Belts will continue to be managed for diverse purposes, chiefly grazing and timber harvest.

Timber harvest is the most critical influence on the Little Belts' natural environment, with annual commercial harvests at 10 million board feet. In the wake of the industrial timber harvest come firewood gatherers, institutionalizing public access to logging roads that might otherwise be closed and revegetated. Demand for firewood has skyrocketed in recent years; estimates are that the amount of cordwood coming from the Little Belts doubles or triples the amount of the regulated timber harvest. In the fall, much of the heavy traffic in the range is trucks and trailers loaded with firewood, bound for Great Falls or Helena woodstoves and fireplaces.

One portion of the Little Belts has at least temporarily been shielded from further roading and timber harvest. The Montana Wilderness Study Act, passed by Congress in 1977 to reserve a handful of areas across the state for possible wilderness designation, included the 90,000-acre Middle Fork of the Judith Study Area. It has not officially been designated wilderness, largely because the U.S. Forest Service recommended that it not be. However, until Congress acts to release the area from protection as a wilderness candidate, the Forest Service is obliged to protect its wilderness values.

Supporters of the Middle Fork of the Judith Wilderness Study Area cite the importance of an unaltered watershed that is source to the Judith River, the only year-round stream flowing from the east end of the Little Belts into the arid reaches of central Montana. This largely roadless area also gives sanctuary to a herd of 1,200 elk, important as an indicator of ecological health and highly touted by hunting enthusiasts across the state.

Milky white cliffs, pockmarked by caves like huge chunks of Swiss cheese, buttress the Middle Fork's channel as it leaves the mountains, cutting through limestone deposited 300 to 400 million years ago and eroding tortuous escarpments on either side. Above the canyon, the river travels through a huge bowl of wild forest, nine by 16 miles, blanketed by Douglas fir at lower elevations and lodgepole pine atop the ridges.

Although a road – actually little more than a wide trail – leads to a parcel of private land at the river's headwaters, the Middle Fork of the Judith remains unquestionably wild. Elk, deer, bear, cougar, lynx, golden eagle and prairie falcon find healthy niches comparable to those in any

of the state's designated wildernesses. A pure strain of native cutthroat trout inhabits the upper portion of the Lost Fork of the Judith. Elk planted in the area in 1915 and 1928 remain among the most prolific in Montana, raising one calf to maturity for every two cows in the herd.

The study area's northern boundary cuts across Yogo Peak and a mining area first developed in the early 1880s for placer gold deposits. By the 1890s prospectors noted blue pebbles among the washed gravels of their diggings, considered them little more than a curiosity and discarded them. By 1898 an English company took control of the claims at Yogo Gulch and developed a gem mining and milling operation, which survives today under different ownership and on a smaller scale. Yogo Gulch once was the premier gem-mining area in the United States, and the Yogo sapphire remains world renowned.

North from Yogo Gulch, the towns of Monarch and Niehart were built and destroyed by the value of silver. Many of their structures are historic relics of the boom days, but the few homes, cafes, bars and stores that survive benefit not from mining, but from the trade of tourists traveling the major highway through the Little Belts en route to places like Glacier National Park. In winter, even more people pass through on their way to downhill skiing facilities at King's Hill at the top of the divide.

The activities of those who go to the Little Belts to work and play weigh heavily on the forest. If the natural integrity of the range is to endure, critical decisions will have to be made to control those uses in the future. The Forest Service has a big job ahead of it.

Above: In the Little Belt Mountains near Utica. Right: "Jake Hoover's cabin," Little Belts. C.M. Russell "partnered" with Hoover in the Little Belts, trapping and hunting from the original Jake Hoover cabin. This is a faithful reconstruction.
BILL KOENIG PHOTOS

ranges of the yellowstone

The commercial airliner heading south from Billings to Denver flies above Bad Pass alongside Bighorn Canyon, the overland trail used by Stone Age residents of the area. Prehistoric cairns placed at frequent intervals still mark its length.

The airplane takes off from Billings, Montana's largest urban area. As it circles above the airport, the grand panorama of the Yellowstone Basin stretches below: to the west are the headwaters of the Yellowstone River, the Continental Divide and Yellowstone National Park across the border in Wyoming. The western view is rimmed by the dramatic peaks of the Crazy Mountains, rising more than 7,000 feet from valley floor to alpine pinnacles. To the south is the massive Beartooth Plateau, a wall breached

Vision-quest site in the Bighorn Mountains. CHARLES KAY

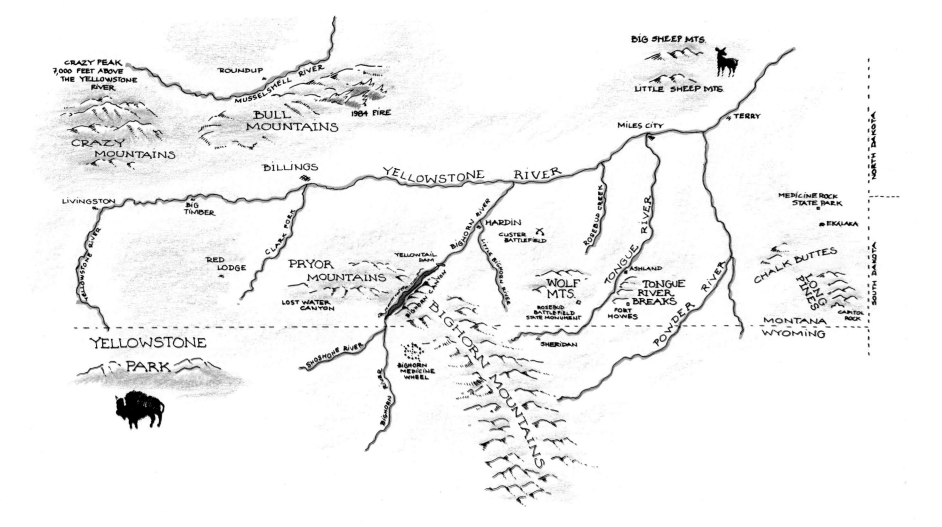

by the broad valley of the Yellowstone River. To the north, the rolling massif of the Bull Mountains appears like marbles under the carpet of the High Plains. Beyond the Bulls, barely a ripple on the eastern horizon, the Sheep Mountain badlands near Terry hem the breaks of the lower Yellowstone.

The airplane turns onto its course for Denver, passing over Montana's southern border. Verdant river bottoms spread out like the veins on a leaf through low, intermittently forested plateaus that stretch hundreds of miles east of the Rockies. Like fingers of a hand laid across the border, with the palm in eastern Wyoming, five rivers water the Yellowstone: the Clark's Fork, Bighorn, Tongue, Powder and Little Missouri. Separating the tributaries are the ridges they have carved: the Pryor, Bighorn and Wolf mountains, the Tongue River Breaks, Chalk Buttes and Long Pines.

No greater contrast in landscapes can be found in Montana than across this broad stretch, from one end of the Yellowstone Basin to the other. At one extreme, the Crazies' jagged peaks and talus heaps mirror the mainstem ranges of the Rocky Mountains. Nearly every alpine cirque cups a pristine high-country lake. Rivulets and creeks fall from every crevice and canyon: the Crazies are marked by the luxury of water. In contrast, 300 miles east across the breadth of the

Famed mountain man Jim Bridger criss-crossed the ranges of the Yellowstone Basin. COURTESY MONTANA HISTORICAL SOCIETY

basin, the Sheep Mountains are a low-slung maze of near-desert canyons, arid and parched, a landscape more like those found in Arizona or Nevada. Between these extremes are the island ranges in a stairstep sequence toward the Continental Divide – not mountains in the classic sense, but prominent rises carved by river erosion, some of them no more than a thousand feet higher than the surrounding plains.

The Long Pines and Chalk Buttes are long, forested tongues of land rimmed here and there by brilliant white cliffs, the northern reach of a prairie archipelago extending from the Black Hills of South Dakota. The breaks of the Tongue and Powder rivers rise and fall abruptly over a space of 75 miles on the highway between the towns of Busby and Broadus. Geologists describe the country as a "dissected plain," in which the sandstone strata of the earth lie exposed like slices of layer cake. The steeply eroded maze of canyons is capped by the coal-baked, hardened sandstone and the well-rooted canopy of a ponderosa pine forest.

To the west, on the sparsely populated Crow and Northern Cheyenne reservations, are the Wolf Mountains (also called the Rosebud Mountains), an undulate ridgeline rising 1,500 feet. Here the westerly progression of increasing moisture and elevation becomes distinct. Bubbling creeks flow year-round, while luxuriant shrubs, grasses and thick evergreen forest soften the angular sandstone cliffs.

West of the Wolf Mountains, the country rises abruptly to the 10,000-foot crags of Wyoming's Bighorn Mountains. The northern end of the

range drops like the top of a half-folded card table, angling into Montana for ten miles. The Bighorn River has gouged the mountainous slab of the Bighorns into a canyon as dramatic as any in North America, though much of it is inundated by the impoundment of Yellowtail Dam on the Bighorn River.

In its final step before the main Rockies, the land rises from Bighorn Lake to the 8,000-foot subalpine meadows of the Pryor Mountains. The Pryors are similar in nearly every way to the main Rockies but are separated from them by the broad valley of the Clark's Fork River.

These dissimilar and far-reaching geographical forms encompass the Yellowstone Basin, a country that long has been agricultural land. Most cattle ranchers still operate on the unaltered rangeland of their pioneer ancestors, using methods that have changed little in a century.

Though energy development is not new to the basin, the rate of energy development accelerated dramatically in the last 15 years (particularly in the 1970s), as coal became more important to the national energy policy. The energy boom made Billings, with 70,000 residents, the state's largest city and the financial center of coal and oil development, irrigated farming and cattle ranching. Since the late 1970s, Montana's production has leveled off, and even dropped somewhat, because of lagging demand. Nevertheless, the Yellowstone Basin continues to be the source of most of Montana's coal production; much of that development has been in or near the basin's mountain ranges.

Island Mountains in Yellowstone Basin History

The Yellowstone Basin is rich with signs of past human communities, some dating back thousands of years. Abundant collections of lithic sites and artifacts from Montana's prehistory are found in the hills that lie south of the Yellowstone— pictographs, tipi rings and hearths, vision quest cairns and pishkuns, or buffalo kill sites. Hunters of bison, antelope and deer, gatherers of roots and plants, the people who created these sites depended upon stone tools such as knives, scrapers and choppers; spear and arrow tips were carefully worked in chert or obsidian.

Before they secured the horse, Indians wounded or killed bison by stampeding them over cliffs. Sometimes the lumbering beasts were coaxed into box canyons that formed natural traps. The hunters leapt from crevices in the canyon wall and thrust their stone-tipped spears at the confused or injured beasts. When blood was drawn, the hunters trailed the wounded animals for miles, awaiting the death of their diet's mainstay. The technique used topography to great advantage.

The Plains Indian ascribed spiritual values to mountains like the immense Bighorns. Just over the border in Wyoming, atop 10,000-foot Medicine Mountain, the roseate glow of the rising sun falls on a circle of stones: the Bighorn Medicine Wheel, a cathedral, calendar and celestial observatory of the Plains Indian.

Above: All the Bighorn Mountains once were Crow Indian country. The range extends well into Wyoming, and is shown here just east of Lovell.
TOM DIETRICH
Left: Just across the Montana border in the Bighorns is an archaeological relic known as the Medicine Wheel, spokes of rock formed into a pattern about whose meaning modern man can only speculate. MARK MELOY

Barely two weeks before the famous defeat of Colonel George A. Custer, Sioux chief Crazy Horse fought General George Crook to a stand-off in the Battle of the Rosebud in the Wolf Mountains. This is the Rosebud Battlefield State Monument. KRISTI DuBOIS

The Crow Tribe probably more than any other people who occupied what was to become Montana attempted to maintain peaceful relations with the advancing white man. Many resent the flooding of their sacred Bighorn Canyon by Yellowtail Reservoir, completed in 1968. TOM DIETRICH

The wheel is 40 feet in diameter and has seven donut-shaped cairns, one in the center and six along its circumference. Twenty-eight spokes of stone cobbles radiate from the central cairn. The wheel is highly revered by contemporary tribes such as the Crows. For centuries their ancestors have used the site for fasting and vision quests. A continuation of that tradition is nearly impossible, as the site is served by a major Wyoming highway and attracts many tourists.

Some archaeologists suggest that the 28 spokes represent the days of the month and that the wheel served as a calendar. In 1972, astronomer John Eddy theorized about relationships between the stone pattern and the celestial paths of the sun and stars. In the chilly glow of dawn on June 21, the day of the summer solstice, Eddy witnessed the alignment of the sunrise with two prominent cairns. Again, at dusk on that day the sun set along the same marker, but at its opposite end. Eddy also confirmed alignments corresponding to the cosmic paths of four prominent stars of the night sky. The Bighorn Medicine Wheel is seen as an archaeastronomical site, one used by sophisticated observers of nature to indicate summer's beginning. Beyond Eddy's theories, little is known about the wheel.

The Crow Indians are the Plains people who occupied much of the Yellowstone Basin when white explorers first arrived. Of Siouan linguistic origins, the Crows came to the area in the 17th century, having been pushed from their native land in the Great Lakes region.

With eloquent simplicity, Chief Arapooish described the Yellowstone country to a Rocky Mountain Fur Company trader, Robert Campbell, in the mid-1800s:

"Crow country is good country. The Great Spirit has put it in exactly the right place; while you are in it you will fare well; whenever you go out of it, whichever way you travel, you fare worse. If you go to the south, you have to wander over great barren plains; the water is warm and bad and you meet with fever and ague. To the north it is cold; the winters are long and bitter and there is no grass. You cannot keep horses there and you must travel with dogs.

"The Crow country is in exactly the right place. It has snowy mountains and sunny plains, all kinds of climates and good things for every season." (Mark H. Brown, *The Plainsmen of the Yellowstone*.)

The European trappers who invaded the Yellowstone Basin in the 19th century called the Indians "Absarokas," or "the bird people," and finally the Crows. In *Montana: A History of Two Centuries*, historians Michael Malone and Richard Roeder state that the Crows welcomed whites as allies against their hostile neighbors, the Blackfeet and the Sioux.

For Francois Antoine Larocque, a British Hudson's Bay Company trader who gave one of the earliest reliable accounts of Crow country (1805), the land was as rich with wildlife as the rest of the region, but strangely harsh. "It is amazing how very barren the ground is . . . nothing can hardly be seen but those Corne de Racquettes [prickly pear cactus]." Traveling with a band of Crows who were camped near the Powder River on their return from a trading expedition to a Mandan village on the lower Missouri River, Larocque said, "Our horses are nearly starved. There is grass in the woods but none in the plains which by and by might with more propriety be called hills. . ."

Lewis and Clark

A year after Larocque, members of the Lewis and Clark Expedition passed through this area. On their homeward journey in 1806, Captain William Clark led a contingent to explore the Yellowstone, moving downstream to meet Lewis's party at the river's mouth. Soon after they entered the basin, half their horses were stolen by some Crows. Clark's men already were building cottonwood-log canoes to float down the river; now, even more men boated than rode. The Crows soon stole their remaining horses, but otherwise the float was pleasant. On August 3, Clark carved his name and the date on what he called a "remarkable rock" that he named "Pompey's Pillar" for Sacajawea's son.

In his journal, Clark noted that the mouth of the Bighorn River would be a "good place for fort & c [*sic*] here the beaver country begins." Fort Manuel, the first permanent structure in the basin, was constructed there in 1807, by Manuel Lisa. He and his party of fur traders were the first really to explore the Yellowstone Basin. During the next half-century, other trappers would follow their paths into every nook and cranny, trapping beavers or trading with Indians.

One member of the Lewis and Clark Expedition would stay in the Yellowstone Country for four years. When the expedition headed for St. Louis in 1806, John Colter remained to trap on the Yellowstone. A year later he hired on with Manuel Lisa's party of trappers (which included another Lewis and Clark veteran, George Drouillard) as they proceeded up the Missouri River.

Later, traveling alone on foot during winter from Fort Manuel at the mouth of the Bighorn, Colter made a particularly arduous trip with a 30-pound pack, a gun and ammunition. Colter did not leave written records and historians can only guess his route. But his description of thermal phenomena at today's Yellowstone National Park earned him a contemporary reputation as a great liar. And, testifying to the southern extent of his travels, a field stone overturned by a plow near Jackson, Wyoming, in 1931 bore the inscription, "John Colter 1808." Back in Missouri two years after his trek, Colter added his conjectured route to Clark's map of the Northwest, published with the expedition's journals.

The fur traders used an important route along the rim of Bighorn Canyon, which separates the Pryor and Bighorn mountains. Called Bad Pass, the cairn-marked trail had been used for thousands of years by natives traveling between the Great Basin and the Northern Plains.

Mountain men like John Colter and Jim Bridger used Bad Pass in their travels to the fertile beaver grounds of Wyoming. They returned with loads of pelts through the rough confines of the canyon and floated the goods down the Bighorn to the Yellowstone.

Midway through the 19th century, the attentions of the mountain men turned from beaver to buffalo. Early sport hunters were quickly replaced by commercial operators who only needed the arrival of the railroad in

The little Bighorn River Valley from the Custer Battlefield National Monument.
TOM DIETRICH

served as fishing-fly tier) and 112 horses. The group is reported to have killed 105 bears, 2,000 buffalo and 1,600 deer and elk.

The 1860s ushered in the wagon-train era. From certain vantage points on the lower slopes of the Pryors and Bighorns, vestiges of what was known as the Bozeman Trail, or Montana Road, still can be seen on the prairie skirting the mountains. It was charted by John Bozeman in 1863. Travelers on the trail constantly were harrassed by Sioux Indians, who objected to the intrusion on their prime buffalo hunting grounds. Despite the danger of attack, about a thousand wagons skirted the Bighorn and Pryor mountains, headed for the newly discovered gold fields in southwestern Montana, but the trail was blocked in 1864 by angry Sioux warriors.

The government sent out military troops in an attempt to keep the Bozeman Trail open. In 1865 they parleyed with Sioux chief Red Cloud and agreed not to build any more roads, forts or settlements along the trail. In turn, the Indians would guarantee safe passage to the wagon trains. The promise was entirely hollow. Ignoring the new treaty, the U.S. Army promptly built three new forts: Fort Reno, Fort Kearney and Fort Smith. Fort Smith was built of logs and adobe blocks where the Bozeman Trail crossed the Bighorn River. It was abandoned three years later when the trail was closed because of Red Cloud's repeated attacks on wagon trains. Incensed by fraudulent treaties, the Sioux and Cheyenne stopped the flow of white immigrants overland.

The irascible Jim Bridger sought and established an alternate route

1881 – for more efficient transportation of hides – to complete the full-scale eradication of the Yellowstone Basin bison. By 1884 the last bison in the east end of the basin were being tracked down and slaughtered from the hidden arroyos of the mountain terraces.

The abundance of wildlife in the Yellowstone Basin before the arrival of commercial hunters was grossly exploited in 1854 when the aging Jim Bridger led Irish sportsman Sir St. George Gore into the country surrounding the Tongue and Powder rivers. In the name of sport, the nobleman's entourage included 27 wagons and a carriage, 40 frontiersmen and several servants (among them Gore's personal valet, who

Left: Hotel at Ubet, 1893, one of many communities that sprang up to provide services to homesteaders.
Below: Homesteader or "honyocker" pushing alfalfa with rake in Yellowstone Valley. COURTESY MONTANA HISTORICAL SOCIETY

and to settle them on reservations. The Crows and other tribes friendly to the U.S. government fought with the whites against the Sioux, Cheyenne and their allies. The confrontations climaxed with the defeat of Colonel George Armstrong Custer on the Little Bighorn in 1876.

Custer's fatal encounter with the Sioux (and others) had begun several years before, with a "scientific" expedition into a sacred land of the Sioux culture, the Black Hills. On that journey in the summer of 1874, Custer shot a whooping crane and a grizzly bear. An equally endangered Plains Indian would later unleash one final act of defiance on Custer and the U.S. Army.

Otherwise relatively uneventful, Custer's Black Hills venture would turn out to be a catalyst to unifying the scattered Indians against the white invasion of Indian territories.

Custer's men returned from the Black Hills with exaggerated stories about treasures of gold. Within four years, nearly 10,000 miners had trespassed onto the sacred Black Hills. The enraged Indians headed west and congregated south of the Yellowstone River.

Disregarding government orders to return to their Dakota Territory reservation, the Sioux and their allies remained in Montana. In the

to the Bozeman Trail. Known as the Bridger Cut-off, the trail edged south of the Sioux hunting grounds and entered the Yellowstone Basin along the Clark's Fork of the Yellowstone. Rough and primitive, without sufficient forage for straining oxen, that trail was soon abandoned.

By 1869, when the Union Pacific Railroad arrived in Utah bolstering supply lines to the frontier from the south, the Yellowstone saw less traffic. Meanwhile, Red Cloud and his warriors burned the abandoned Fort Smith and reclaimed the hunting grounds they reluctantly shared with their enemy the Crows.

Custer at the Little Bighorn

The 1870s brought the military back to the basin on various campaigns to defeat the Plains Indians

spring of 1876 the U.S. Army plotted a campaign to surround the errant Sioux and subdue them.

In March 1876, General George Crook attacked a large Indian village on a tributary of the Powder River. The battle was inconclusive, since most of the Indians escaped capture and were able to retreat to a larger encampment to the north. Crook and his cohorts called it their victory, but the battle little more than stirred the bees' nest. On June

the Wolf Mountains, proceed down the Little Bighorn River, then await the arrival of other forces. Instead the impetuous Custer chose to disobey the orders and on June 24 proceeded on an all-night march directly into the Sioux camps. Custer topped the last hill above the Little Bighorn and saw an enormous congregation of Indians–perhaps 20,000 people, an encampment that stretched for five miles. Indians from a thousand tipis were celebrat-

nerable by luck. "At worst, by assaulting this congregation of feathered savages he would lose his life and the lives of everybody who followed him," Connell writes. "A less disagreeable script included failure, accompanied by the humiliating necessity of defending himself until Gibbon and Terry arrived." The third possibility may have been what blinded him to his folly. In it he foresaw his regiment "scattering the most dangerous horde of Indians

in the valley beyond. Custer shrugged away the advice and proceeded to his doom.

Custer's bloody end actually heralded the final days of the free-roaming Plains Indian. Only months after the Battle of the Little Bighorn, fully one third of the entire U.S. Army had been deployed to Montana Territory to crush the Indian rebellion. By the following spring, thousands of Indians had been rounded up and returned to the reservations. The Yellowstone Basin was made ready for white settlement. Even the reservation of the Crow, allies of the white army, suffered successive reductions in size as the region was opened for cattle grazing.

XIT Ranch cowboys at supper beside Hungry Creek Springs, 1904.
COURTESY MONTANA HISTORICAL SOCIETY, L.A. HUFFMAN, PHOTOGRAPHER

17 the Crook forces proceeded down Rosebud Creek to a camp in the Wolf Mountains, where Sioux chief Crazy Horse attacked by surprise. Twenty-five soldiers were killed, and Crook returned to Fort Fetterman in Wyoming, for new orders and reinforcements. The Rosebud fracas set the stage for the battle that occurred a week later on the Little Bighorn River.

Traveling west in advance of the command of General Alfred Terry, General Custer had not heard of Crook's defeat. His Seventh Cavalry was to ride up the Rosebud, cross

ing their recent victory over Crook on the Rosebud. The gathering not only included the Sioux and Cheyenne, but Indians from four other tribes, each in a separate circle of tipis.

Some historians have suggested that Custer's decision to attack the enormous encampment was nothing short of mass suicide. Others suggest that, once detected, the troops had little choice but to fight, no matter the odds. Evan S. Connell, in *Son of the Morning Star*, believes that Custer's choice came from a delusion that he was made invul-

ever gathered on the American continent. If that should be so, then he–-George Armstrong Custer–would ride in triumph through the streets of Washington like Alexander through Persepolis."

Custer and his entire command–-211 men–lay disemboweled in the prairie heat a half hour after the bugler sounded attack. Had he taken the advice of his Crow scouts, the massacre would have been avoided. From an outpost atop the Wolf Mountains later venerated as the "Crow's Nest," the scouts could see the immensity of the Indian forces

Vast open-range herds arrived from Texas and Oregon in 1881, and within four years the eastern half of the Yellowstone Basin had become the stockman's undisputed domain, where a million head of cattle, sheep and horses roamed the hills between the Bighorns and the Dakota border. At the time, it was not unusual for a single operator to claim 50,000 to 100,000 animals. Many were foreign investors struck by the productivity of the Montana prairie. "A herd of 5,000 head will feed the year round and grow fat on a stretch of arid-looking table-land," said an Englishman surveying the lower Yellowstone in the 1880s, "where an English farmer, if he saw it in autumn, would vow there was not sufficient grazing for his children's donkey." (Quoted by historian Robert Athearn in *High Country Empire*.)

The character of the basin changed abruptly after 1887, when more than 60 percent of the open-range cattle perished during the "Hard Winter of 1886-1887."

XIT Ranch

The open-range operations continued on a reduced scale, as more stable headquarters provided winter feed and care. One of the largest cattle operations was the XIT Ranch. This multi-state enterprise, based in Texas, began when a group of Chicago investors agreed to construct the Texas capitol in exchange for the deed to more than three million acres of Texas rangeland. In 1890 the investors expanded into Montana, acquiring a lease on two million acres near Miles City. Ten thousand Texas cattle were trailed 1,600 miles north to the Yellowstone and turned loose beyond the river.

During the last great days of the open range, much of the lower Yellowstone remained a seemingly endless unfenced grassland. An XIT cowboy could stand atop the 1,000-foot rise of the Big Sheep Mountains and spot cattle for miles across the gentle swells of land in both the Missouri and Yellowstone basins. Often the cattle would find shelter behind the badland cliffs of the Sheeps, shade in summer and windblown grass when the country was hit by blizzards.

More than 200 XIT cowboys, served by five supply wagons, rode herd on more than 15,000 animals. Every fall for almost two decades, the herd was rounded up, and fat calves and steers were shipped to Eastern markets. The XIT ordinarily shipped five batches of cattle requiring two trainloads each.

Laid off during the winter months, the cowboys drifted from ranch to ranch, supported by odd jobs and absorbing as much social life as they could–mostly dances. "Girls were very scarce and any cowboy who managed to spear himself a steady girl was considered a cut above the rest, or he usually felt that way anyhow," according to J.K. Marsh, an XIT cowhand whose story was told in *Montana the Magazine of Western History.* "It was very seldom that a school marm taught the second term without annexing some cowboy for a husband, and as a rule they had the entire bunch to choose from."

By 1909 cowboys like those on the XIT were permanently out of jobs, as much of the undeeded land was taken up by homesteaders lured west by laws that encouraged settlement and by the exaggerated advertising of the railroads. After the Enlarged Homestead Act of 1909, anyone could claim deed to 320 acres of Montana land after living on the property for three years. To make the prospect all the more enticing, the Northern Pacific Railroad placed large billboards along its rights-of-way showing a farmer plowing silver dollars across a map of Montana.

Would-be farmers claimed 42 percent of the entire Montana land base between 1910 and 1922, though only 20 percent of that land was even suitable for farming. Seventy percent of the land claimed was in eastern Montana. "Hunyak," or honyocker, a pejorative term for Slavic immigrants, became the generic name for all the homesteaders. Journalist Joseph Kinsey Howard, in *Montana High Wide and Handsome,* describes them this way: "Honyocker, scissorbill, nester . . . he was the Joad of a century ago, swarming into a hostile land: duped when he started, robbed when he arrived."

Most of the people who came to Montana to farm survived a few years, only to return home after they had exhausted their savings. Few accounts tell the stories of those

Some of our far eastern badlands and mountains were ridden in 1886 by Teddy Roosevelt when he ranched in North Dakota. MONTANA HISTORICAL SOCIETY

who failed; they simply came and went in anonymity. The tale of a family who settled east of the Bull Mountains was written by William Kilgour, a young man who endured the ordeal of the honyocker, in *Montana the Magazine of Western History.* "It was required that you build a house and live in it for three years, hoping that the land you selected would be bountiful," Kilgour wrote, remembering the days when land was free but difficult to hold. "If there was no water you had to dig a well or have it dug. Often there was no timber and you had to go miles, even for firewood. Usually there was no herd law and you had to build fences to protect your crops from range cattle. If you did raise a crop, you had to haul it many miles to the closest market and sell it for whatever it would bring at the moment. Stakes were big in your gamble with the weather. In the long run, the homesteader paid dearly for the land — only some survived the ordeal."

The Kilgour family survived barely five years in the Bull Mountains. Gradually they were forced to take other jobs to make ends meet, and eventually William joined the Army when all hope for the farm was lost. When he returned to the farm at the end of his tour of duty, everything of any value had been stolen from the property, including the fences. Kilgour sold the land his father had homesteaded and moved on to a new occupation. "A land that started with cattle has gone back to cattle," was his resigned conclusion.

ranges of the yellowstone

Montana's Yellowstone River is one of a handful of great American rivers that have survived most of the 20th century with a curious and rare status: remaining undammed. Flowing free across southern Montana for more than 400 miles, the great river defines a huge geographic province known as the Yellowstone Basin. It is fed by cerulean lakes in Wyoming's high country, and nearly all its tributaries intersect Montana's southern border. The mainstem emerges from Yellowstone Park, and east of it run the Clark's Fork, Bighorn, Tongue, Powder and Little Missouri rivers. Between each's tributaries are the island-like

In the Crooked Creek drainage, Pryor Mountains. MARK MELOY

basin - today

Bighorn Bull Crazy

Pryor Sheep and Wolf Mountains

Tongue River Breaks Chalk Buttes

Long Pines and Ekalaka Hills

mountains and terraces: the Pryor, Bighorn and Wolf mountains, the Tongue River Breaks, Long Pines and Chalk Buttes.

With the exception of the Shields River and Big Timber Creek flowing from opposite sides of the Crazy Mountains, no major tributary enters the Yellowstone River from the north side of the basin. The long dry ridges of the Bull and Sheep mountains separate the Yellowstone and Missouri basins.

Tongue River Breaks

You might expect a Hollywood hero such as Gary Cooper, John Wayne or Gregory Peck to emerge from its purple sage, riding a gray stallion to the top of a layer-cake mesa. It is not Arizona's Monument Valley, a national park or even a wilderness area. It is a rather anonymous piece of public land known as the Ashland District of the Custer National Forest, or simply, the Ashland Forest.

It is unmistakably cowboy-movie country–rough broken prairie, lush creek bottoms, mesa-top mosaics of stately pines and grasslands. Its singular claim to fame may be that Western novelist Louis L'Amour named a novel *Hanging Woman Creek,* for a verdant canyon on the west end of the Ashland Forest.

This is a silent land, sparsely populated. Those who live here preserve traditional rural lifestyles. The continuous operation of a ranch by five generations of one family is not uncommon on the creeks and terraces draining the Tongue River between Ashland and Decker just north of the Wyoming border.

The Ashland Forest tops an ancient plateau of a half-million acres between the Tongue and Powder rivers. Like a huge layer cake whose edges have been nibbled ragged by hungry mice, wind and water erosion have laid bare steep arroyos at its base, creating a maze of canyons

known as the Tongue River Breaks. The brittle sandstone walls disintegrate over time, blown away in a whirlwind of grit, further steepening the canyon walls. Great chunks of crumbly stone fall to growing heaps of sand at the bottom, exposing distinct bands of deposition–earth tones of sand and clay, seams of jet-black coal and the reddish-pink of clinker (sandstone baked to the hardness of pottery by burning coal seams). Millions of years of geologic history are laid bare across the 50-mile-wide plateau rising barely a thousand feet above the prairie floor.

The breaks' steep canyons have been severely undercut by erosion, forming enclaves or small caves — haunting spaces protected from the elements. Those sheltered hollows of sand were for 10,000 years the sites of Stone Age communities. Caves set back in sandstone walls contain layer upon layer of the de-

Rancher Mark Stevens at Fort Howes on Otter Creek in the Tongue River Breaks.
MARK MELOY

Right: Petrified stump in pine hills near Decker, which is in theTongue River Breaks.
KRISTI DuBOIS
Far right: View of the Tongue River Breaks north of Ashland.
CONNIE WANNER

bris of human settlement, neatly preserved by veneers of finely sifted sand, as yet scarcely touched by trained archaeologists. For the most part these ancient people were desert foragers who lived on grubs, roots and small animals.

Today's residents of the breaks country favor comfortable but austere ranch homes along sheltered creek and river bottoms. Atop a conspicuous knob of sandstone at the head of Otter Creek is an odd stone structure, a small stockade built of unmortared chunks of flat rock. Rancher Mark Stevens' home sits immediately below the rock hut. Stevens tells you the story of a frontier confrontation between settler and Indian–the story of Fort Howes and the fight that might have happened.

When Stevens' great-grandfather, former sea captain Calvin Howes, came to this country in 1880, there were only five permanent ranches south of the Yellowstone River in Montana, Stevens says. Howes' choice of land was on Otter Creek in the heart of that forested plateau country. The location was dubbed Fort Howes in 1896, when Calvin's son Levi and others erected the stone stockade atop a hill above the ranch. Though the "fort" saw no battles, it was a symbol of settlers' expectations of Indian attacks.

Instead of fighting Indians, the settlers sometimes fought among themselves. In 1901 the *Yellowstone Journal* of Miles City reported that 11 masked men clubbed 200 sheep to death on Tooley Creek, one of several confrontations between sheepmen and cattlemen who competed for grazing on the open range.

In 1907 these large-scale stockgrowers petitioned Congress to establish a forest reserve to regulate grazing. Not only did the new system settle grazing squabbles, it restricted further homesteading of that rangeland. The ranchers were satisfied to have a system that perpetuated their vested interest in the public land.

Today, 20,000 cattle graze the reserve, now a part of the Custer Forest. Only the major creek bottoms are narrow corridors of private land, with ranch headquarters and hay fields that produce feed for cattle pulled off the forest from November to May.

Above: In the Medicine Rocks State Park. JAN WASSINK
Right: Eerie sandstone formation in Medicine Rocks was probably eroded by wind. KRISTI DuBOIS
Far right: The so-called Long Pines area in the Custer National Forest. KRISTI DuBOIS

Though ranchers maintain perpetual grazing rights on the forest, the land is available to public use and enjoyment. It is a vast but little-used area for driving, horseback riding and hiking. Several roads cross the forest, graveled with dusty reddish-pink scoria rock. Ranchers who make frequent trips to town consider air-conditioned cars a necessity, so thick is the road dust. The evergreen trees along the road are tinted by the fine red dust showered upon them by passing cars. No one ventures far after a rainstorm, as the otherwise firm road surfaces turn to gelatin-like, gumbo mud.

Despite the mud and dust, a drive up to Poker Jim Flat is worth the effort. The elevation gain catches enough moisture to water meadows thick with prairie flowers. Rambling for miles, the meadows are heaven for cattle and deer and pleasant

enough to cause some cowboys to forget their work and relax. One cowboy "relaxed" into a game of poker a century ago and was caught by his boss. The cowboy, Jim, left without a job but his name stayed. Or so the legend of Poker Jim Flat goes.

The country is described as "breaks" for good reason. At the edge of the great plateau, the land dives into a jumble of eroded V-shaped gullies. Terrain too rough to attract many visitors, it does occasionally entice cattle or game down into the canyons to use the small springs that trickle from walls of rock but are promptly soaked up by the sandy soils.

The ponderosa pines that thrive atop the plateau are stunted and gnarled in the canyon bottoms, where they compete for precious moisture with green ash and other shrubs. Gradually the environment gives way to bunchgrass, and a

desert environment of juniper and sagebrush. Poker Jim Creek makes its way through this tortuous sandstone maze–not really a creek until it flows as a trickle from one puddle to the next where the canyon fans out toward the Tongue River.

The country's fascination seems to come from its untouched loneliness; it is a place where one could camp and not see anyone for weeks at a time. The management plans of the Custer National Forest set aside a tenth of the Ashland District for hiking and horseback recreation-- 40,000 acres in three small roadless areas that include the land surrounding Poker Jim Creek. "Physically challenging recreational activities would center around coping with a harsh environment in the summer as well as the winter," the 1985 draft plan said of the area's recreation potential. "Poisonous snakes are

common inhabitants offering the challenge of coexistence. Hiking trails as such are nonexistent." With that kind of promotion the place could likely stay unpeopled.

But the future wilderness quality of two of those small roadless parcels may be compromised by a coal mine planned on adjacent private land. The peace and seclusion of Poker Jim Creek will be eradicated by the massive draglines of an open-pit mine scraping enough coal from the earth to fill an estimated 800 box cars a day.

The price of progress will be severe to the Tongue River Breaks, if and when this Montco mine is built. The more hopeful locals like to think that the ancient character of the land will endure; the near-desert prairie inspires that kind of optimism.

Capitol Rock in the Long Pines is named for its resemblance to the nation's Capitol building. MARK MELOY

Ekalaka Hills, Long Pines and Chalk Buttes

Ekalaka. The syllables drop from the tongue like a primitive chant. It is an Oglala Sioux word and the name of a modern community, the center of government, population and culture for the extreme southeast corner of Montana. A journalist once wrote in a history of Carter County, "Ekalaka isn't the end of the world, but it is the end of the road." Today, the pavement ends just south of the town whose reputation is synonymous with the word remote.

Ekalaka was founded in 1885 by a buffalo hunter who set out to erect an "edifice for the eradication of ennui," according to the local wisdom of a signboard just outside town. The hunter's wagon bogged down in snow, and there the community was founded. "Hell," exclaimed the founding father, "any place in Montana is a good place for a saloon," so he unloaded and built right there.

The Carter County Museum is enough reason to come to Ekalaka. Constructed of building-block-sized chunks of petrified wood, it houses an eclectic collection of frontier and natural history: the oak cabinetry of a 19th-century small-town post office, a whiskey still that saw commercial production not too many years ago in Carter County, a thousand-pound triceratops skull, a reconstructed skeleton of a duck-billed dinosaur and hundreds of knick-knacks–the random archives of rural Montana.

Few people simply pass through Ekalaka or go there on a lark, yet the country around it contains some of the most spectacular scenery in eastern Montana, public land atop three island-like, verdant terraces of the Sioux District of the Custer National Forest.

Popping up immediately south and east of Ekalaka are two sets of buttes. Stark white cliffs, 300 feet high, rim the Chalk Buttes and Ekalaka Hills with sandstones deposited in the Oligocene period of geologic history. The stone is extremely soft and crumbly, and often whole cliffsides fall and further steepen the rims, presenting the brilliant white of newly fractured rock. On a clear day, it is said, the cliffs are visible from North Dakota, South Dakota and Wyoming.

A dozen miles farther east, the Long Pines rise 700 feet above the prairie floor between Box Elder Creek and the Little Missouri River where it flows into South Dakota. Beyond that the Short Pines of South Dakota complete a prairie archipelago breaking the otherwise even plains north of the Black Hills. In the Long Pines is an isolated outcrop of white volcanic ash that bears uncanny resemblance to the nation's capitol. The formation's name is appropriate since it and its environs belong to the U.S. government: Capitol Rock is a protected monument administered by the Forest Service, which controls nearly 150 square miles of ponderosa-pine forest among the three islands of Carter County.

Those forests are a haven for white-tailed deer and Merriam turkeys, a game bird planted there in the 1950s. In none of the bluffs will the rush of a running stream be heard. Most of the springs trickle only short distances before they are soaked up by porous sandstone.

Tie Creek along the southern border of the Long Pines is a channel remnant of wetter times, so named when timber was cut for a railroad in the 1880s. The idea was to float the ties down the Little Missouri, whence they could be hauled by barge down the Missouri River. Those tie timbers that ran aground along the shallow Little Missouri inevitably propped up many an early homestead.

Supporting rich mosaics of wildflowers and an anomalous tree, precious water in the Long Pines is found in places like Lantis Spring, named for an early-day sawmill operator, and Plum Creek, which in May is adorned with the white-blossomed thickets of wild plum, chokecherry, strawberry and Oregon grape. Seemingly out of place here

are paper birch trees, which normally grow in a colder climate with more rainfall. The trees are thought to be relicts of a time when the climate of southeast Montana was vastly different.

The high cliffs of the terraces and surrounding lush fields of grain and grasslands provide a raptor's rapture–hundreds of eagles, hawks and falcons nest in the limestone crags. Forest Service biologists claim that the area is remarkable for its diversity of raptor species and is world-renowned for its concentration of the rare merlin falcon.

View from the limestone cliffs of the Ekalaka Hills. MARK MELOY

According to local legend, the spirit of the Crow and Sioux Indians who resided in the area is kept alive by the hawks and eagles soaring past the white-crested buttes. Amid the weird sandstone formations of what is now Medicine Rock State Park north of Ekalaka, native hunters gathered in the fall. It was a place of fasting and prayer to summon the "medicine" or spirits that would protect the men as they went to hunt buffalo.

Indian legend also gave names to landmarks in the Chalk Buttes. The clearly unscalable angular column of rock called Starvation Butte is said to have been climbed by an Indian woman whose footing crumbled beneath her as she pulled herself to the top. Unable to return, she died of starvation atop the butte. Fighting Butte was the site of a skirmish in which a hunting party of Crows was chased to the butte's top by Sioux. Backed to the steep edge of the table of rock, the Crows were forced to leap to their deaths when their enemy set the prairie ablaze.

Sitting near an old cabin in a sequestered corner of the Chalk Buttes, a place as remote as any Montana has to offer, I hear the surreal chortles of tom gobbler wooing his mate. From the cliffs above, a cluster of swooping falcons dive at a hatch of evening insects, and deer graze at the meadow's edge. Rancher Bill Blair brought me here to see the splendid reflection of the prairie sunset on the high white cliffs.

When asked what people from this country of serene beauty did on their days off, Bill replied with a twist of irony in his voice, "They go to Billings."

Pryor Mountains

Mountain man Jim Bridger charted a trail into Montana in the 1860s and guided parties of military men

and settlers along it. The Bridger Cutoff entered Montana at the state's south-central border and skirted the massive Bighorn Mountains and the impenetrable forests of the Yellowstone Plateau. The route brought wagon wheels down the Clark's Fork of the Yellowstone in the shadow of a range dubbed the Pryor Mountains in honor of Nathaniel Pryor of the Lewis and Clark Expedition.

The town of Bridger, 20 miles from the Wyoming border, was named for the nearby ford where Bridger's wagon trains crossed the Clark's Fork River. Today, a road from Bridger–part of it the old Bridger trail–is a main access point to public land in the Pryors.

From Pryor Gap, a low prairie pass east of Bridger, the landscape is dominated by an 8,500-foot reef of limestone that seems like a petrified tidal wave rushing in the direction of Billings 30 miles north. The Pryors are quite simply a double ridge about 20 miles across, breaking off into low timbered buttes to the north. They are a backyard recreation area for the most populous area of the state, Yellowstone County and Billings.

The National Park Service manages public land along Bighorn Canyon National Recreation Area on the east end of the Pryors. To the south, the Bureau of Land Management has charge of a wild-horse range. The Forest Service manages the high country of the Pryors, and the northern buttes lie on the Crow Reservation.

Timber harvest and grazing in much of the Pryors take second place to resource management objectives emphasizing recreation and natural preservation. Most tourists enjoy the Pryors from a distance, usually from a boat on Yellowtail Reservoir in Bighorn Canyon. More adventurous visitors drive 35 miles of dirt road from Bridger to a picnic area known as Big Ice Cave.

Big Ice Cave is an underground chamber the size of a small auditorium. Its ice floor remains frozen through the summer, insulated by the thick cave walls. The cool subalpine climate outside the cave supports stands of Douglas fir, lodgepole and limber pine. In springtime the high meadows are colorful palettes of white phlox, scarlet shooting stars, blue pasque flowers and yellow violets. Industrious prairie pocket gophers, nature's rototillers, keep the meadows spongy and aerated.

That near-alpine environment contrasts sharply with the desert environment just 10 miles south and 5,000 feet lower in elevation. The top of the ridgelines collects 20 inches of moisture a year, while the drylands below are lucky to gather seven inches. Crooked Creek, the only perennial stream flowing from the backside of the Pryors, is the boundary of the 37,000-acre Lost Water Canyon roadless resource, accessible to only the most committed hikers.

Lost Water Canyon contains a dozen separate ecosystems ranging from subalpine to desert prairie. As a rare, unaltered "edge" environment, where the Rocky Mountains meet the Great Plains, it is extremely important as a natural area. At the junction of Crooked Creek and Lost Water Canyon, the topography appears to be a gently sloping plateau, with meadows of bunchgrass and sagebrush, as the higher-elevation Douglas fir merge with lower-elevation ponderosa pine. The deep vertical canyons at the confluence of the two creeks attain a height of 800 feet, dropping straight down like huge cracks in the limestone massif of the Pryor Mountains.

Above left: Mule deer in the Sheep Mountains. MARK MELOY

Above left: The remote and rugged Chalk Buttes near Ekalaka. KRISTI DuBOIS
Left: Chalk Buttes in autumn. TOM DIETRICH
Above right: The Pryor Mountains' Crooked Creek Canyon. MARK MELOY
Above: Limestone cliff in the Pryors. MARK MELOY

Top: The Pryor's Big Ice Cave is an oasis of cool air in a nearly desert mountain environment.
Bottom: The thick walls of the cave keep its floor frozen year 'round.
MARK MELOY PHOTOS

This web of sinuous canyons on the south flank of the Pryors long has been a barrier to human use and development. The Forest Service calculates that the area experiences only 50 visitor days a year — a generous estimate. Few, if any, of these visitors actually decend into the canyons. Those who do find the going difficult in the thick, brushy canyon bottoms.

As important as the Pryor Range is as a natural area, public attention has focused on the Bureau of Land Management's Pryor Mountain Wild Horse Range. Animal lovers from all over the country make pilgrimages to the lower stretch of the south flank of the Pryors hoping to catch sight of the wild horses, 129 head in 1984.

Designated in 1968 as the nation's first wild-horse range, the reserve covers nearly 50,000 acres. The horses are biologically and historically important: They are thought to be the descendents of the original stock of Spanish horses brought to North America in the 17th century and to the Pryors by Indians in the 1700s. Controversy over the horses' origin stems from the fact that early trappers recorded no observations of them.

Whether an authentic biological relict species or simply feral horses of questionable lineage, the horses nevertheless are inspiring, running wild and free at this prairie edge of the Rockies.

Sheep Mountains

To a geologist the Sheep Mountains are not mountains. To the residents of Prairie County north of the Yellowstone River, the long narrow sandstone ridge is a prominent geographic divide.

The Sheep Mountains form a spine of "gumbo hills" dividing the Missouri and Yellowstone rivers east of Miles City. If you dumped a bucket of sand on a table and sprayed it with a hose so that steep channels cut into its sides, you would create a likeness of these highland features.

The 50 miles of gravel road between Brockway and Terry pass alongside the high point of Big Sheep Mountain, a ridge that rises barely a thousand feet above the prairie. The Sheep Mountains receive slightly more moisture than the surrounding plains and are thick with grasses and prairie wildflowers by the middle of July.

Named for their original inhabitants a hundred years ago, the ridge was thought to provide ideal shelter from the harsh winds of winter. The frontier herder could watch his flocks over a large area from a shelter in the sandstone wall.

The crest of Big Sheep Mountain is softened by a blanket of heather-like shrubbery that is actually dwarf juniper, commonly found on wind-blown ridges in eastern Montana. A ground cover no more than a foot high, it grows on hundreds of acres on the north face of the ridge. Buff-colored cliffs with bands of gray, black and red enclose plant thickets of the green ash and chokecherry community–wild plum, buffalo berry, serviceberry and rose hips, the spartan fruits of the prairie.

The Sheep Mountains are habitat for mule deer. In the springtime the blossoms of ubiquitous forbs — phlox, pasque flower, star lily, musineon, primrose, dandelion – are ideal muley diet, along with the succulent new leaves of buckbrush, silver sage and threadleaf sedges. As prime mule-deer range, the Sheep Mountains have been studied by the Montana Department of Fish, Wildlife and Parks. The studies show a great variation in the numbers of deer from one year to the next, ranging from 180 deer in 1976 to 1,200 in 1983 in one study area. In 1985 biologists noted that the population at the same site had dropped 40 percent from the previous year. The reduction was part of a game-management program calculated to reduce habitat overcrowding. In the previous hunting season officials had permitted harvest of up to six deer per hunter to thin out the herds and protect range conditions in the Sheep Mountains.

The increase of deer in Prairie County has been inversely proportional to its human population. Since 1930 the county has lost nearly half its residents. Most of them were homesteaders busted by the financial calamities of the '20s.

The failure of small farms on the arid rangeland left nearly half of the county's million acres to the government, which now leases it to local stockgrowers through the Bureau of Land Management and a countywide cooperative grazing district, the largest in the state. Grazing on all lands of the county, private and public, is controlled by the district's supervisors. "Socialism," one rancher calls it facetiously.

All told, hoofed animals outnumber people 25 to one in Prairie County. Yet the Sheep Mountains appear remarkably free of signs of overgrazing. They constitute a little-known piece of wild prairie in Montana, perhaps destined to remain unchanged.

Bighorn and Wolf Mountains

The Bighorn Mountains are sacred to the Crow Indians. Tribal legend says that a Crow named Scarface ran into them when he was a boy, seeking refuge after his face was badly burned when he fell into a campfire. There he constructed the Bighorn Medicine Wheel (in present-day Wyoming) and used the site for a vision quest. He returned to become a medicine man.

Another parable is recounted by Henry Old Coyote, in Edwin C. Bearss' *Bighorn Canyon National Recreation Area, Montana-Wyoming: History Basic Data.* A boy and his stepfather went into the Bighorns to hunt at a place called Hole-in-the-Wall. On the brink of a steep canyon, evil spirits entered the man and made him push his stepson from a steep cliff to certain death. When he returned to the village, he reported that the boy had lost his way in the forest. A search was unsuccessful.

The boy had fallen into some cedars growing from the canyon wall and survived. On this perch hundreds of feet above the rocky talus of the narrow canyon, he sat four days. Nearly dead of hunger and exhaustion, he finally was rescued by a band of seven bighorn sheep led by Big Metal, with hooves and horns of glistening steel. Big Metal gave his own name to the boy and each of the six other sheep gave him a power — wisdom, sharp eyes, sure-footedness, keen ears, great strength and a strong heart.

Big Metal returned to his people bearing a sacred message. The sheep had told him, "We seven rule these Bighorn Mountains. That river down there is the Bighorn River. Whatever you do, don't change its name. If you ever change the name of the river there will be no more Absaroga [Crow Tribe]. The Absaroga will be nothing."

In 1968 the river that cascaded down the narrow canyon flanking the Bighorn Mountains became a 17,000-acre lake plugged by the 525 vertical feet of concrete of the Yellowtail Dam. Much of Big Metal's canyon home is now the domain of cabin cruisers, water skiers, swimmers, an occasional paddler and 19 species of fish. The Crow remain in the country, but they are vastly different than the Absaroka of a hundred years ago.

The wide, gently sloping band of mountains projects from the west side of Bighorn Lake like a tongue emerging from a mouth whose teeth are the crags of the Wyoming Bighorns. For 20 miles the lower north end of the Bighorns extends into Montana onto the Crow Reservation. That land is also the largest piece of contiguous land wholly owned by

Above: The road over Sheep Mountain Divide from Brockway to Terry. Below: Big Sheep Mountain. MARK MELOY PHOTOS

the tribe, a vestige of the vast frontier once entirely their domain. Today the reservation encompasses nearly 2.3 million acres, 30 percent of which is owned by non-Indians. Of the Indian land, 80 percent is leased to non-Indian ranchers.

Because the Bighorns, as well as the Pryor and Wolf mountains, also on the reservation, are sacred places to be used for religious purposes, 79 percent of that land is untouched stands of virgin timber. Tribal members may camp and hunt in the mountains year around; non-Indians must secure a tribal permit to enter them.

Most outsiders see the fabulous canyons of the Bighorns from a motorboat on the waters behind Yellowtail Dam. Sheer canyon walls, many a thousand feet high, are an effective barrier to exploration beyond the lake's shoreline.

Though constant hunting pressure has severely reduced some wildlife, biologists have found 79 species of mammals, 260 varieties of birds and 19 different kinds of reptiles and amphibians in the canyon environs of the Bighorns. Three endangered species, bald eagles, peregrine falcons and whooping cranes, have been sighted periodically in the Bighorns. The Crow tribe maintains a herd of buffalo in the Bighorns, harvesting some of them each year.

The people of the Bighorn country carefully and proudly maintain the traditions of their culture. Andrew Birdinground, whose great-grandfather served Plenty Coups, the last great chief of the Crow, continues to prepare pemmican from dried buffalo meat and berries from the high slopes. Where once the meat was ground with stones, today steel meat grinders are used. The pulverized

Top: The Rosebud Valley and the Little Wolf Mountains north of Lame Deer.
JIM ROMO

Bottom: The Wolf Mountains. MARK MELOY

meat is mixed with lard or salt pork, chokecherries, June berries and wild plums.

Another Crow, Marvin Stuart, describes the significance of fasting. In the past, tribal leaders went to the mountains to fast and procure good fortune for their people, sometimes returning with a prophecy of the tribe's future. The leader then offered direction to avert problems and danger. These days, fasting is more personal, according to Stuart. People fast in hopes of bringing protection to themselves and relatives, particularly to avert illness or to help someone who is sick.

As contemporary life brings rapid cultural change, traditional fasting and dancing are losing importance. The Christian denominations win more tribal members each year, discouraging the converts from participating in many of the traditional Crow ceremonies, Stuart says.

Stuart is an expert on the development of tribal resources. The Wolf Mountains, he says, lie atop one of the richest deposits of coal in Montana–billions of tons of coal beneath reservation land. Royalty payments to the tribe from leases at the Westmoreland Mine already have helped finance new employment opportunities and education projects. Further coal leasing and development, according to Stuart, would do much to solve the tribes' chronic unemployment rate, which often tops 70 percent.

Five huge tracts in the Wolf Mountains have been leased to energy developers. Only Shell Oil, according to Stuart, is ready to construct a new mine near the Wyoming border. Difficulties in obtaining surface access to some of the land and the current low demand for coal have stalled the project. Nevertheless, large-scale resource development appears to be in the future of the Wolf Mountains.

"The Crows have always been friends to the white man," Marvin Stuart noted. Many served as scouts for the U.S. Army in the 1870s. A century later the Crows are still friendly to the corporations of the "yellow eyes," as Stuart calls whites. Stuart always will remember the words of his grandfather, who once said, "Keep an eye out for the white man. If you have something they want, they will eventually get it." People like Stuart intend to be around to make sure that the white man pays for what he gets from the Indian.

Bull Mountains

The low-slung, 50-mile-long Bull Mountains massif seems like a ruffled blanket of dark ponderosa-pine forest laid across the eastern Montana prairie. Its buff-colored cliffs isolate the cowtown of Roundup from another world: Billings, Montana's largest city, 50 miles to the south. The Bulls' sandstone terraces also separate the basins of the Missouri and Yellowstone rivers and provide only thin, ephemeral tributaries to the Musselshell River as it etches a circuitous channel north of the range, making its way to the Missouri.

Fire's leading role in the formation of the Bull Mountains is evidenced in the bands of black coal and reddish sandstone along the crumbling tan cliffs.

The grassland terraces of the Bulls were a favorite haunt of aging bull bison unable to migrate with the rest of their herd. The Indians who tracked them considered the Bull Mountains a place to hunt when

other game was hard to find.

A thousand springs of crystalline water emerge from the steep cut-banks of sandstone, flowing along broad coulees claimed by a handful of cattle ranchers. Less than five percent of the range is public land, and nearly every crest and rill of the Bull Mountains is lined by primitive private roads. Most people see little more of the Bull Mountains than the views afforded from a speeding car along the paved road that bisects the range between Billings and Roundup.

Roundup is a durable little town of 2,000 people on the timbered breaks of the Musselshell River, where the sandstone terraces drop abruptly to the river. Established by the commerce of coal miners who labored to fuel the engines of the Milwaukee Railroad, Roundup has survived for a century the industrial coming and going of railroads, oil and coal. One wry old-timer offered his sentiments

Top: *The low-rising mass of badlands north of Billings known as the Bull Mountains.* **Above:** *The Bulls suffered a devastating fire in 1984.* MARK MELOY PHOTOS **Right:** *What looks like a massive thundercloud is actually smoke from the "Roundup Fire" in the Bulls as seen from the Snowy Mountain area.* TIM MILBURN

Above: The Campbell strip farms at the foot of the Bighorn Mountains. MARK MELOY

Right: View to the east overlooking Bighorn Canyon National Recreation Area. CHARLES KAY

about Roundup's future: "With the coal and oil booms gone, fortunately, there is nothing left to save Roundup."

More than a decade ago, Roundup's economic boosters had high hopes for the development of huge new underground coal mines in the Bull Mountains. The large-scale mines have failed to materialize, while coal from the Bulls serves little more than to heat homes around Roundup.

The area's economy was spurred by the development of several subdivisions in the Bulls in the 1970s. In late August 1984, about 50 of those homes were destroyed by the huge Hawk Creek forest fire, and everyone learned a blunt lesson in forest ecology. The fire burned a quarter-million acres in the range, the largest of more than 300 separate fires that ravaged Montana in the dry summer of 1984 and prompted Governor Ted Schwinden to proclaim: "Our state is literally on fire." The fire raged for weeks, only to be extinguished by autumn rainstorms.

A year after the fire, Gene Cole still poked through the ashes of his belongings. The fiery blast swept through like a napalm bomb and left his home looking like an abandoned war zone.

Twenty-five tons of possessions — a lifetime's accumulation of tools, electronic gear, computers and a library of 7,000 books — lay in an eroding heap of damp cinders. Cole kicked out a warped brass oarlock, the remains of his son's rafting equipment. "When we first got here, it was all green and pretty. It's lost that beauty now. You see only charred sticks where once there was a forest."

Formerly a Navy electronics technician, Cole arrived with his family a short time before the fire. A small fortune in building materials was ready for construction on land adjacent to his father's home. The Coles lost everything to the fire. They had no insurance.

Gene Cole's remembering was particularly painful as he stood by the gutted foundation of what was once his father's comfortable home. His father, Owen Cole, died of a heart attack after the futile battle to block the fire at the edge of his 70-acre plot.

"I haven't come up here very much. You can tell I get pretty disgusted," Gene Cole said. "The land is worth only half as much, and half the people have moved out. But we're the optimists. We intend to stay and start over as best we can."

Others suffered differently as nature cleared the prairie of timber. At the head of Fattig Creek, the fire spared the ranch house of Steve Charter's family by virtue of the home's location in a large meadow away from billowing flames feeding on dry boughs of ponderosa pine. But the fire did not spare their fences. Without fences, a ranch effectively ceases to be. Charter also lost 75 yearling cattle, and the feed from 13 sections of grazing land was gone as winter approached.

Charter spent five sleepless nights fighting the fire, which a fellow rancher called "one you could fight all you wanted but weren't going to beat." Despite his losses, Charter remains optimistic. "This type of thing was bound to happen," he said. "Ever since this country was settled, we have been putting out fires. The Bull Mountains ultimately became a tinder box ready to ignite. In the long run it will do us good because the country needed to be cleared of scrub timber. The fire will create

more grassland and we should see more water in our springs since the trees are no longer there to consume it."

Summer rainstorms in 1985 drenched the ground with enough moisture to encourage everyone that the three-year drought was over. Nutrients borne by the ash of the fire had begun the work of rejuvenating the land, and the sod beneath the charred canopy had sprouted a vibrant green cover. From the limbs and trunks of the eerie blackened trees came a ceaseless noise, grinding, chewing, like the rush of a stream: burrowing insects reducing the standing dead to sawdust. When the light of day is low, the tiny particles of wood seem to sparkle in the hollow spaces of the blackened forest.

Near the place where he found the remains of his young cows, Steve Charter also came upon a flock of dead turkeys, curiously unsinged by the fire that killed them. Apparently they suffocated when the flame passed through the tree tops consuming the oxygen and superheating the air below.

According to State Department of Fish, Wildlife and Parks biologist Tom Butz, a considerable number of wild animals died in the fire. "The ones that weren't consumed directly by the flames died the following winter when forage was in short supply," he said. "The turkeys will recover because they are so prolific, hatching 10 to 12 fledglings in the spring. They did particularly well this summer [1985] because there were a lot of grasshoppers around, and turkeys love 'hoppers.'"

The deer in the Bull Mountains will take longer to recover because they are not nearly so prolific, and drought conditions before the fire

Yellowtail Reservoir from Devil Overlook. CHARLES KAY

had left them particularly vulnerable. "Deer numbers were going down in a hurry before the fire," Butz said. Of particular concern were the mule deer occupying the dry terraces away from the Musselshell River. Based on aerial counts of the last five years, the number of fawns per adults was plunging. There were six to seven fawns for every 10 adults before 1983; after the fire only two to four fawns per 10 adults were counted. Butz estimates that half of those fawns were consumed directly by the flames, while the adults more likely escaped the inferno.

As the summer after the catastrophic fire brought a pronounced "greening up" in the Bulls, their future looks considerably brighter. Rancher Steve Charter, small businessman Gene Cole and biologist Tom Butz all agree that things have to get better in the Bulls. They can hardly get worse.

Crazy Mountains

"It's a good country. Where a man can sit his saddle and see. . . all across to the west stretch the Crazies, and, swinging in the stirrups, a man has to throw back his head to follow their abrupt shoulders up to the white crests of the peaks. A pretty clean country where a man can see a long way and have something to see." So wrote Spike Van Cleve in *Forty Years' Gatherin's.*

Nowhere else in Montana is the transition from prairie to mountains so dramatic. Over the space of 20 miles, from the low terraces of the Yellowstone River to the top of Crazy Peak, the landscape rises 7,000 feet. Said to be one of the largest exposed sections of igneous rock in the world, the Crazy Mountains reach an elevation over 11,000 feet above sea level. Sharpened by glaciers and honed by wind and water erosion, sawtoothed ridges radiate from the oval-shaped range.

Fully half the range is composed of nearly vertical peaks and rock slides at the bases of broken cliffs. The exposed, rocky terrain, however, is not without plentiful water. Alpine basins support lush coverings of vegetation, and 40 high-country lakes — only 15 of which are named – are fed year-round by snowfields. Water rushes through cascading streams, forming the headwaters of the Musselshell to the north and the Missouri to the west. The Shields River and Sweetgrass Creek flow from opposite sides of the range to water the Yellowstone.

Fifteen miles across and 30 miles wide, the isolated Crazy Mountains cover only 136,000 acres and seem nearly half as tall as they are wide. They mark the horizon from great distances. Early travelers, in fact, used them to measure their progress up the Yellowstone Valley. Some say the Crazies even got their name by popping up in the craziest places on the central Montana horizon: you will be wrapped in the gentle undulations of the prairie, then suddenly, this grand bulge of land breaks up from the horizon.

Other tales say that the wall of mountains was named when a woman settler was separated from her wagon train and wandered into the mountains. She could not survive the isolation and the rugged terrain without going mad, so the range was dubbed the Crazy Woman Mountains. The name apparently stuck, although it was later shortened.

Today people flock to the Crazies for hiking and backpacking; the precipitous terrain has kept the Crazies pristine and essentially roadless. A popular hike across the range is a three-day backpack in which the hiker must surmount two switchback passes, each rising over 2,000 vertical feet, in a space of five air miles. Along that route are seven spectacular mountain lakes nestled in great alpine cirques, where a reclusive mountain goat or two may be seen.

One early "hiker" came to the Crazies to fulfill a spiritual need not unlike that of Moses climbing Mount Sinai. Plenty Coups, last great chief of the Crow Indians, sought a vision in the Crazies in 1857 with which to lead his people.

At age 10, Plenty Coups came to the mountains to fast and dream and perform the traditional rites of passage into manhood. So strong was his desire to be a great leader of the tribe that he chose to seek his vision on the highest peak of the ragged Crazy Mountains. He purified his body in a sweat lodge at the lake below the mountain then climbed upward. On the summit he roamed until he dropped from exhaustion in a bed of "ground cedar and sweetsage" and lay for four days until at last his dream came.

In his vision, Plenty Coups saw the great herds of buffalo vanish from the plains below him, to be replaced by a strange spotted animal he did not recognize. When his vigil ended, the boy was carried from the mountain top by his tribesmen and returned to camp to recount the vision's details.

Elders interpreted Plenty Coups' vision to portend the end of the buffalo and the predominance of the white man's spotted cattle on the Great Plains. Accepting the omen, Crow leaders sought to ally themselves with the white settlers and welcomed their arrival. Except for a few minor skirmishes, the Crows never went to war against Montana settlers. Such was the result of Plenty Coups' vision in the Crazies.

One of the first non-Indians to climb Crazy Peak was geologist John E. Wolff in August 1889. He later wrote, in a report to the U.S. Geological Survey, "They are one of the most interesting localities in the world for igneous rock . . . scenically I have never seen in such small compass, beautiful waterfalls and cascades and peaks." Fellow geologist Ranney Lyman added, "The preeminent feature of this ruggedness is Crazy Peak . . . The birdseye panorama was of surpassing grandeur. Billowy clouds floated over the landscape; the changing lights and shadows emphasized the rugged detail of the rough terrain, and alternately concealed and exposed in flashing brilliance, the many lakes like deep set gems."

It is a great tragedy that much of this mountain range, a national treasure, was lost from the public domain in 1865 when the Northern Pacific Railroad received from the U.S. Congress "checkerboard ownership" in the Crazy Mountains. As incentive to build the railroad finally completed in 1883, the federal government gave the corporation every other section of land for 20 miles on either side of its right-of-way. That land not only made the Northern Pacific the largest private landholder in Montana, it also gave the railroad title to some 50,000 acres (about half) of the Crazy Mountains.

To finance construction and operation of the railroad, that land was sold and today belongs to six individuals and corporations. Thus many peaks and pristine mountain lakes in the Crazies remain private property. To say the least, the checkerboard situation of ownership has made it difficult for the U.S. Forest Service to administer its share of acreage in the Crazies for the benefit of the public.

Under considerable public pressure, the agency continues its efforts to reacquire the land through land trades for federal properties outside the range. To date that effort has been as unsuccessful as have private-sector efforts to develop new roads and homesites within the Crazies. Meanwhile the standoff has given the Crazies' wildness a tenuous lease.

Left: Lofty alpine settings worthy of the Rocky Mountains far to the west characterize the high country of the Crazies. This is Upper Twin Lake at sunrise.
Above: Falls on Big Timber Creek. CHARLES KAY PHOTOS

Opposite page: No other range brings inspiring mountain-scapes to the prairie as do the Crazy Mountains. TIM CHURCH

At Zortman, Little Rocky Mountains. Fireweed in foreground. TOM DIETRICH

Bibliography

Abbott, Edward Charles (Teddy Blue). *We Pointed Them North.* New York: Farrar & Rinehart, Inc., 1939.

Bearss, Edwin C. *Bighorn Canyon National Recreation Area, Montana-Wyoming: History Basic Data, Vol. 1.* Office of History and Historic Architecture, Eastern Service Center, National Park Service, Department of the Interior, February 1970.

Bennett, Ben. *Death, Too, for the Heavy Runner.* Missoula, MT: Mountain Press Publishing Company, 1980.

Coburn, Walt. Quotation from *Pioneer Cattlemen of Montana,* by Walt Coburn. Copyright 1986 by the University of Oklahoma Press.

Connell, Evan S. Excerpted from *Son of the Morning Star,* Copyright © 1984 by Evan S. Connell. Published by North Point Press and reprinted by permission. ALL RIGHTS RESERVED.

Frantz, Joe B. "Texas' Largest Ranch— in Montana: The XIT." *Montana the Magazine of Western History* 11 (Autumn, 1961): 46-56.

Guthrie, A.B. From *These Thousand Hills* by A.B. Guthrie, Jr. Copyright © 1956 by A.B. Guthrie, Jr. Reprinted by permission of Houghton Mifflin Company.

Howard, Joseph Kinsey. *Montana High, Wide and Handsome.* Copyright 1943 Yale University Press.

Hutchens, John K. *One Man's Montana.* Philadelphia: Lippincott, 1964.

Kilgour, William. "The Nester." *Montana the Magazine of Western History* 15 (Winter, 1965): 37-51.

Malone, Michael P. and Richard B. Roeder. *Montana: A History of Two Centuries.* Seattle: University of Washington Press, 1976.

Montana Historical Society Staff, comp. and ed. *Not in Precious Metals Alone.* Helena: Montana Historical Society Press, 1976.

Price, Con. *Memories of Old Montana.* Hollywood: The Highland Press, 1945.

Sharp, Paul Frederick. *Whoop-Up Country.* Minneapolis: University of Minnesota Press, 1955.

Stegner, Wallace. From *Wolf Willow.* by Wallace Stegner. Copyright © 1955, 1957, 1958, 1959, 1962 by Wallace Stegner. Reprinted by permission of Brandt & Brandt Literary Agents, Inc.

Stuart, Granville. *Forty Years on the Frontier: Prospecting for Gold* (Vol. 1) and *Pioneering in Montana* (Vol. 2). Lincoln: University of Nebraska Press, 1977.

Van Cleve, Spike. *40 Years' Gatherin's.* Kansas City: Lowell Press, 1977.

Next in the Montana Geographic Series

Montana's Flathead River Country
Its North Fork comes from Glacier Park Country. Its Middle and South forks emanate from the heart of the Bob Marshall Wilderness. The lake that shares its name is a national magnet. It is the Flathead River system and its significance to Montana is profound. This book tells of its natural history—the wildlands, the waters, the wildlife; and its human history—how the Flathead Valley was settled, steamboats on the lake, the cherry industry. And you'll visit the beautiful Flathead country today—see communities as diverse as Polebridge, Bigfork and Kalispell, learn about recreation on the lake and the river, and follow the little-known part of the river from Kerr Dam to the Clark's Fork River. By Bert Gildart, author of *Montana's Missouri River*, and co-author of *Glacier Country* and *Montana's Wildlife*—all books in the Montana Geographic Series.

Montana's Homestead Era
The homesteader was a pioneer in a wave of settlement that embodied much of the American dream: land to be had merely by "proving up." "Honyockers" or nesters, as they were called, were lured by the thousands by outrageous descriptions of what the Montana prairie would bear. In a few years, most would be defeated and gone, and the landscape would never be the same. Their story is part of the Montana lore, part of the state's character. Dan Vichorek, Montana Magazine columnist, has set out to capture the color, the promise and the heartbreak of that time—as much as possible through the stories of the living homesteaders themselves.

The Montana Geographic Series:

Volume 1: Montana's Mountain Ranges
Volume 2: Eastern Montana: A Portrait of the Land and the People
Volume 3: Montana Wildlife
Volume 4: Glacier Country: Montana's Glacier National Park
Volume 5: Western Montana: A Portrait of the Land and the People
Volume 6: Greater Yellowstone: The National Park and Adjacent Wild Lands
Volume 7: Beartooth Country: Montana's Absaroka-Beartooth Mountains
Volume 8: Montana's Missouri River
Volume 9: Montana's Explorers: The Pioneer Naturalists
Volume 10: Montana's Yellowstone River
Volume 11: Montana's Indians, Yesterday and Today
Volume 12: Montana's Continental Divide
Volume 13: Islands on the Prairie: The Mountain Ranges of Eastern Montana

Each volume is $13.95 plus $1.25 for postage ($15.20 total)

Discounts are available through our
Montana Geographic Series Subscription.

Montana Magazine

Tells the Whole Montana Story

The history, the wild back country, the people, the wildlife, the towns, the lifestyle, the travel—these things are Montana—unique among the states. Montana Magazine brings you the Montana story six times a year in a beautiful, long-lasting magazine. Its hallmark is full-page color photography of Montana from the peaks to the prairies.

Regularly Featured Departments

Weather
Geology
Hunting and
 Fishing
Outdoor
 Recreation
Humor
Personality
Dining Out

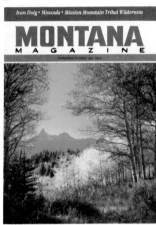

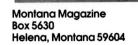

Montana Magazine
The Most Complete Guide to Enjoying Montana

$15/year - 6 issues
$27 for 2 years

Montana Magazine
Box 5630
Helena, Montana 59604

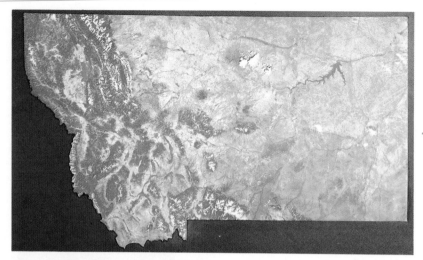

About Our Back Cover Photo

This photographic mosaic was compiled from Earth Resources Satellite Photo passes made from a height of 570 miles. It was pieced together in black and white and interpreted in color by Big Sky Magic, Larry Dodge, Owner. Commercial Color Adaptation © 1976 Big Sky Magic.

Front Cover photographs

Clockwise from bottom left:
From "The Knees Hills." John Reddy.
Square Butte. Jim Romo.
Snowy owl. Robert Brewer.
Bearpaw Baldy. Robert Brewer.
Bearpaw Mountains. Chuck Jones.